SJ
9/03

INSTITUTE OF LEADERSHIP & MANAGEMENT ilm
SUPERSERIES

Managing Change

FOURTH EDITION

0

Published for the
Institute of Leadersl

OXFORD   AMSTERDAM   .RIS
SAN DIEGO·   SAN FRAN(TOKYO

Pergamon Flexible Learning
An imprint of Elsevier Science
Linacre House, Jordan Hill, Oxford OX2 8DP
200 Wheeler Road, Burlington, MA 01803

First published 1986
Second edition 1991
Third edition 1997
Fourth edition 2003

British Library Cataloguing in Publication Data
A catalogue record for this book is available from the British Library

ISBN 0 7506 5879 7

For information on Pergamon Flexible Learning
visit our website at www.bh.com/pergamonfl

Institute of Leadership & Management
registered office
1 Giltspur Street
London
EC1A 9DD
Telephone 020 7294 3053
www.i-l-m.com
ILM is part of the City & Guilds Group

The views expressed in this work are those of the authors and do
not necessarily reflect those of the Institute of Leadership &
Management or of the publisher

Author: Jane Edmonds
Editor: Heather Sergeant
Editorial management: Genesys, www.genesys-consultants.com
Composition by Genesis Typesetting Limited, Rochester, Kent
Printed and bound in Great Britain by MPG Books, Bodmin

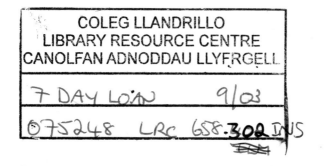

Contents

Workbook introduction   v

  1   ILM Super Series study links   v
  2   Links to ILM qualifications   v
  3   Links to S/NVQs in Management   vi
  4   Workbook objectives   vi
  5   Activity planner   viii

Session A   Change through continuous improvement   1

  1   Introduction   1
  2   What does continuous improvement involve?   1
  3   Tools for aiding continuous improvement   8
  4   The 5S Programme   18
  5   Standards and continuous improvement   23
  6   Summary   31

Session B   Planning change   33

  1   Introduction   33
  2   Reasons for major change   34
  3   Change and the first line manager   36
  4   Preparing for change   45
  5   Planning the project activities   51
  6   Establishing responsibilities and methods of communication   61
  7   Summary   67

Session C   Implementing change and managing its consequences   69

  1   Introduction   69
  2   Monitoring the project plan   70
  3   Completing a change project   75
  4   Summary   82

Contents

Performance checks   83

  1   Quick quiz   83
  2   Workbook assessment   85
  3   Work-based assignment   86

Reflect and review   89

  1   Reflect and review   89
  2   Action plan   93
  3   Extensions   95
  4   Answers to Activities   96
  5   Answers to self-assessment questions   96
  6   Answers to the quick quiz   99
  7   Certificate   101

Workbook introduction

1 ILM Super Series study links

This workbook addresses the issues of *Managing Change*. Should you wish to extend your study to other Super Series workbooks covering related or different subject areas, you will find a comprehensive list at the back of this book.

2 Links to ILM Qualifications

This workbook relates to the following learning outcomes in segments from the ILM Level 3 Introductory Certificate in First Line Management and the Level 3 Certificate in First Line Management.

C4.1   Continuous improvement
    2   Understand techniques for continuous improvement
    4   Understand methods of evaluating continuous improvement activities

C4.2   Planning change
    1   Identify reasons which prompt change
    2   Identify and plan activities to achieve change
    3   Identify and plan resource implications
    4   Identify and plan timescale to achieve objectives
    5   Plan communication and involvement to facilitate effective change

C4.4 Implementing change
1 Implement or co-ordinate planned change as appropriate
2 Identify ways to monitor and control change against plan
3 Revise, plan and reschedule change as appropriate to ensure objectives are met

C4.6 Managing the consequences of change
1 Understand the consequences for the organization of change, or maintaining the status quo
2 Appreciate the 'ripple effects' of change throughout an organization
3 Identify the human and financial implications for the organization, teams and individuals

3 Links to S/NVQs in Management

This workbook relates to the following elements of the Management Standards which are used in S/NVQs in Management, as well as a range of other S/NVQs.

A1.1 Maintain activities to meet requirements
A1.3 Make recommendations for improvements in work activities
B1.1 Make recommendations for the use of resources
C12.1 Plan the work of teams and individuals
C12.3 Provide feedback to teams and individuals on their work

It will also help you to develop the following Personal Competences:

- building teams;
- focusing on results;
- thinking and taking decisions;
- influencing others.

4 Workbook objectives

Today change goes on all around us, all the time. It may once have been enough for a manager to fit into whatever job he or she was given and just keep things ticking along smoothly in much the same way as they always had.

Today, however, no manager can afford to accept the status quo. If an organization is to stay competitive and prosper, it must constantly change – which means that an essential part of your role as an effective manager is to initiate, plan and implement change.

As a first line manager, the type of change you initiate yourself will probably be small-scale, perhaps as part of a gradual, ongoing programme of continuous improvement, in which frequent minor changes are made to processes and products or services. In a small organization, you may also have the opportunity to initiate a larger, more dramatic change that crosses departmental boundaries. But the more likely scenario is that large-scale change projects will be initiated by senior management, often in response to opportunities and threats presented by external forces. Either way, you, as a manager will need to take a major role in:

■ preparing your team for change;
■ planning how a change is to be implemented;
■ monitoring and evaluating what is achieved by the change;
■ dealing with the consequences of change.

In this workbook we will begin by looking at the techniques for identifying possible improvements in day-to-day activities in the workplace. These techniques include a variety of diagrams, such as flowcharts and fishbone diagrams, and procedures for auditing various aspects of the working environment. Underpinning everything is an ongoing process of setting and monitoring standards.

In the case of cross-departmental or organization-wide change, your role may well be that of project manager. Consequently, we will examine some of the basic tools used by project planners, such as critical path diagrams and Gantt charts, and the part they play in the successful implementation and monitoring of change.

Finally, throughout the book we will be considering some of the knock-on effects and consequences of change. As you may know from your own experience, these are not always beneficial. We will look at some of the negative effects as well as the many positive ones.

4.1 Objectives

When you have completed this workbook you will be better able to:

■ initiate improvements in workplace activities;
■ plan change projects;
■ manage the implementation of change;
■ monitor and evaluate change projects.

5 Activity planner

The following Activities require some planning so you may want to look at these now.

Activities 4, 6, 8 and 10 ask you to examine one process in your job where you know there is a lot of room for improvement. It would be helpful to start thinking as soon as possible about what process this might be.

Activities 18a, 19, 20, 21, 32 and 36 ask you to consider various aspects of a past major change project. Activities 18b, 23, 25, 26, 30 and 31 ask you to consider various aspects of a forthcoming major change project. It would be helpful to start thinking as soon as possible about which change projects these should be.

Some or all of these Activities may provide the basis of evidence for your S/NVQ portfolio. All portfolio activities and the Work-based assignment are posted with this icon.

The icon states the elements to which the portfolio activities and Work-based assignment relate.

The Work-based Assignment on page 86 suggests that you plan a forthcoming major change in some detail, preferably with the involvement of your team. The suggestion is that you return to the change identified in Activity 18b (and on which you do further work in subsequent Activities). You might, however, wish to consider another change project, in which case it will be helpful to start thinking about what this project will be.

Session A
Change through continuous improvement

1 Introduction

In today's highly competitive environment, really successful organizations recognize the need not only to provide quality products or services, but also to keep on increasing the quality of these products and services so that they exceed customers' expectations. Organizations ignore the need to focus on quality, at a price customers can afford, at their peril.

So how, in practice, can an organization keep on increasing quality? The answer is through a commitment to a programme of continuous improvement, in which all staff are encouraged to make suggestions on how processes – and consequently products and services – can be improved. As a manager you have a vital role to play, not only in coming up with ideas yourself and encouraging your team to come up with ideas, but also in evaluating ideas and planning how they can be implemented.

In this session we will focus on what is involved in ensuring that continuous improvement goes beyond the ideas stage and becomes a reality.

2 What does continuous improvement involve?

The idea that organizations should aim to improve the quality of their products and services on a continuous basis was first taken up in Japan, where the word for continuous improvement is 'kaizen'. It comes from a book published in 1986 entitled *Kaizen: The Key to Japan's Competitive Success*, written by Masaaki Imai.

2.1 Kaizen

EXTENSION 1
In this workbook we will look at a small selection of kaizen tools. An excellent source of more information on kaizen is Extension 1, *Kaizen strategies for successful organisational change*, by Michael Colenso. You will find more information on Extension 1 on page 00.

At the heart of kaizen is the idea that if customers' constantly changing needs and wants are to be met, there must be continuous improvement in small steps, at all levels, forever. Everyone has a role to play in achieving it, from senior management down to first line managers and their staff. Senior and middle managers need to concentrate on establishing the necessary strategy, structures and systems, and on monitoring what is being achieved. First line managers, on the other hand, need to concentrate on encouraging staff to come up with suggestions for improvements and ensure that these are responded to. This of course means that staff must come up with suggestions and be prepared to change the way they do things and acquire new skills.

Activity 1

5 mins

1   What ideas, if any, have you had in the last week or so for improvements in the workplace? Jot down one or two, no matter how small you think they are.

_____

_____

_____

_____

2   What ideas have your staff had? Again, jot down one or two.

_____

_____

_____

_____

There are all sorts of things you could have written here, but the chances are that they were to do with one of the following:

■ **the physical conditions in which you and your staff work**
These include the layout of your workplace, and environmental factors such as noise, lighting, temperature and ventilation.

■ **the resources you and your staff work with**
Resources can range from money, to equipment, machines, tools, vehicles, materials, information and people.

■ **the relationships you have with other people, both within and outside the organization**
'Other people' can include suppliers, customers, colleagues, the people you manage, and managers at higher levels than yours.

■ **the procedures you and your staff follow**
For each part of your job there will be particular step-by-step procedures you are supposed to follow – or there may be a marked absence of procedures. Established procedures are not always the best, and a lack of any agreed procedure can sometimes result in chaos.

Activity 2

3 mins

Have a look at the ideas for improvements you jotted down in Activity 1. Try putting each one into one of the four categories listed below.

Physical conditions

_____

Relationships

_____

Resources

_____

Procedures

_____

Here's an example of how one manager's job can generate numerous ideas for improvement in all four categories.

Uma is the Publications Officer for a medium-sized charity. Among her responsibilities is the production of a bi-monthly, four-page newsletter for staff and regular contributors. It is only a small item, but it takes up far too much of her time, diverting her attention from her other responsibilities, which range from producing press releases to organizing the editing, design and printing of training packs. One of the two editors who work for her, Sam, has the job of getting all the material together to pass on to an external designer. This not only includes text from contributors within the organization, many of whom seem to have no idea about deadlines, but also photos the quality of which the designer often complains about.

All too often Sam gets into a panic over the need to meet the design and printing schedule and has to turn to Uma for help. Not only this, but he distracts the other editor, Gemma, from what she is doing. She sits right next to him and can't help but listen in to his harassed-sounding phone calls and then take a look at what he is doing, either on the screen of his word-processor or on the manuscript or proofs lying on the small clear space on his desk or, more usually, on the floor.

When Uma looks at this situation she can see a range of ways in which it could be improved. Starting with physical conditions, it's clear that having Sam and Gemma sitting right next to each other is not the best layout for their office. They need to consider how they can make better use of the available space, while at the same time ensuring that both of them get sufficient light.

In terms of resources, Sam has all the basic computer equipment he needs, but he is short of something very basic: desk space. When they consider how best to rearrange the office they will also need to consider the possibility of changing some of the fittings and furniture. Another resource they are missing is a good digital camera. The quality of the photos they pass on to the designer is poor because they are often taken by people, Sam included, at a low resolution on cheap digital cameras.

Then there is the thorny problem of relationships. Sam's relationship with both Gemma and Uma is being affected by the fact that he often becomes irritable when he's under pressure. This could be sorted out if the pressures on him were reduced. One of the most obvious things that causes this pressure is the late arrival of contributions to the newsletter – particularly those from senior managers – and the tendency of people to start changing what they have written when they see it on designed pages. A new relationship needs to be established with senior managers, in which they recognize the need to show more consideration to Sam and the Publications Department as a whole. Perhaps they don't even realize what problems they are causing, because the Publications Department doesn't make it clear what it wants.

Finally, there are the procedures they follow. It is obviously not an effective way of putting the newsletter together to have people sending in contributions later than the schedule agreed with the designer, and then – in the general haste to get the newsletter underway – passing on these contributions without editing them properly or cutting them down to roughly the required length.

If Uma was able to make all the improvements that she has identified as necessary, she would be on the way to establishing a really effective process. It would not, however, be a perfect process. In kaizen, there is always room for improvement.

2.2 Process improvement

Let's have another look at Uma's situation and focus on the procedures that are followed in the production of the newsletter. If she can sort these out, she will be well on the way to making the overall process effective.

At the moment, the week after a newsletter is distributed to staff:

- an email goes out to everyone asking them to submit features, and dates for the 'diary section' for the next newsletter by a date no later than four weeks' time;
- Uma approaches one or more members of staff to ask if they will write a short feature on one of the subjects she knows to be of particular interest at present;
- Sam begins collecting a dossier of items for the News section.

The first major problem is that not all the promised material arrives by the date it is due. The second is that if, and when, it does arrive it is often way over the agreed length and requires major cutting – which in turn means the material going backwards and forwards between the contributor and Sam. Over the course of the week before everything is due to go off to the designer, Sam battles away on his computer to get the material edited and cut to approximately the number of words needed to fill four pages. Because it arrives in bits he has to do this between other tasks. He also often doesn't know what pictures are going to be included and so can't take them into account in his estimated word counts. Inevitably, not all the material goes off to the designer at the same time.

The designer does the best he can with what he's been given. However, when the final bits of text finally arrive, some of it only roughly edited because it's so late, he invariably has to change the layout of one or more pages. There's also the problem with the pictures. These usually come from a number of people, none of whom have the right equipment to take a picture that will reproduce well. This means a lot of phone calls to see if something better can be supplied.

Eventually, the designer gets the newsletter to the stage where proofs can be sent to Sam, Uma and all contributors for their approval. Unfortunately, it's often at this stage that contributors decide they want to totally rewrite something, and Sam and Uma start doing some serious editing. In theory, Uma's only involvement should be to give the newsletter a final check, but she's found too many mistakes in printed newsletters in the past not to get more heavily involved. The net result of all this is that a large number of corrections go back to the designer. Inevitably, mistakes are made in the correction process, and sometimes Sam ends up having to check three or four proofs, often outside official working hours as the deadline approaches for getting the newsletter to the printer.

All this is a huge waste of time and energy. What can be done to eliminate this waste?

Activity 3

4 mins

Imagine you are Uma and are determined to find ways of improving the procedures for producing the newsletter. What ideas do you have? Jot down a couple.

_____

_____

_____

There are a number of things you might consider. To begin with, ideally Sam needs to get all the text on time. Uma knows that in reality it won't always be possible to get the Chief Executive, for example, to submit her contribution on time – but there is no reason why the vast majority of contributors can't do so. They need to be given more information about the various stages in the process. And they need to understand the knock-on effects of submitting text late and then deciding to rewrite it after the newsletter has been designed. Perhaps she should send out an information sheet and hold a series of brief seminars on the subject. At the same time, she could talk to them about the need to either supply high-quality pictures themselves, or be prepared to specify what pictures they would like to see included well in advance, so that Sam can arrange for good-quality pictures to be taken.

Provided Sam receives most of the text on time, he should then concentrate on editing and cutting the text to approximately the right length. If he knows what pictures are going to be included, he can work out their size on the page using a simple formula and then make a more accurate estimate of the number of words that can be fitted into the remaining space. Uma can make the whole thing easier for Sam by scheduling in a chunk of time for him to concentrate on the newsletter, and then reading through the text **before** it goes to the designer. It should then only be necessary to have three proofing stages and a minimal number of corrections – saving a lot of time for Sam, the designer and herself.

Activity 4

| Portfolio of evidence | S/NVQ A1.3 |

This Activity may provide the basis of appropriate evidence for your S/NVQ portfolio. If you are intending to take this course of action, it might be better to write your answers on separate sheets of paper.

Identify one process in your job where you know there is a lot of room for improvement. Write down your first thoughts about the changes that should be made in terms of:

■ physical conditions:

_____

_____

■ relationships:

_____

_____

■ resources:

_____

_____

You will need your answer to Activity 4 for Activities 6, 8 and 10.

■ procedures:

_____

_____

3 Tools for aiding continuous improvement

So far we've assumed that all you need to do in identifying areas for improvement in a process is to:

■ recognize where something is not going as well as it might;
■ think about what the causes are;
■ come up with ideas on how to tackle these causes.

Sometimes this is all you need to do. But in other situations you may need to undertake more careful analysis in order to discover the root cause of a problem. There are a number of tools you can use to help you do this. Here we are going to look at just three:

■ the five whys;
■ process flowcharting;
■ cause and effect diagrams.

3.1 The Five Whys

The Five Whys is a simple technique, developed by the Japanese, which consists of asking the question 'Why?' in relation to a particular process, outcome or event.

Let's take a straightforward example. You come home late one evening and find a stain on the sitting room carpet. You ask your teenage son 'Why did this happen?' Your son replies: 'Because a drink got knocked over.' You ask, 'Why did the drink get knocked over'. He replies 'Because I was fooling around with a couple of friends'. 'Why,' you ask, 'were you fooling around?' 'Because,' he replies, 'we were a bit drunk.' 'And why were you drunk?' 'Because we'd had some vodka as well as a few beers.' 'So why did you drink so much?' 'Because we've just finished our exams and wanted to celebrate.'

If you apply this process to a situation where there's a problem at work, you'll be surprised at how much you can learn about the connections between outcomes and causes. It could take more than five 'Whys' to find out the root cause of something, but usually five is quite enough.

Activity 5

5 mins

Imagine you work for the same charity as Uma. You have written an article for the bi-monthly newsletter and have been told that, no matter how busy you are, you will have to check the proof version and get it back to the Publications Department by the next day. 'Why the rush?' you ask Uma. 'Because,' Uma replies, 'we are way behind schedule.'

Knowing what you do about the Publications Department, try continuing this conversation using the Five Whys technique.

_____

_____

_____

_____

_____

_____

_____

_____

_____

_____

_____

There are a number of ways this conversation could go, but they should all end up with the same root cause. Here is one of them:

- 'Why are you behind schedule?'
- 'Because Sam sent the last section of text to the designer one week later than he was supposed to.'
- 'Why did he do this?'
- 'Because the contributor sent it to Sam very late.'
- 'Why did the contributor send it late?'
- 'Because he didn't make it a priority to get his feature written on time.'
- 'Why didn't he make it a priority?'
- 'Because he doesn't realize how important it is to meet the deadline we set him.'

Once the conversation has reached this point, it's time to consider how to improve the situation.

S/NVQ A1.3

Activity 6 · 8 mins

This Activity may provide the basis of appropriate evidence for your S/NVQ portfolio. If you are intending to take this course of action, it might be better to write your answers on separate sheets of paper.

Go back to the process you made notes about in Activity 4. Select one aspect of the process that is a problem and see whether you can find out the root cause of the problem by using the Five Whys technique. You should end up with a list of a maximum of five questions beginning with 'Why?', plus their answers.

_____

_____

_____

_____

_____

_____

_____

_____

_____

_____

_____

_____

_____

_____

3.2 Process flowcharting

Flowcharts are another tool that can help you to analyse a process and identify areas for improvement or problems and their solutions.

In its most simple form, a flowchart is a list of steps in a process, each of which leads to the next one. Let's return to the example of the production of the bi-monthly charity newsletter. If all goes well, the main steps should be as follows:

1   People invited to contribute text plus suggestions for pictures

2   Contributions arrive

3   Contributions edited and pictures taken/found

4   Edited contributions sent to designer

5   Designer returns first proofs

6   First proofs checked by editor and necessary cuts made

7   Corrections on first proofs implemented by designer and second proofs returned to Publications Dept

8   Second proofs sent to contributors for their approval

9   Second proofs returned to Publications Dept

9   Corrections on second proofs implemented by designer and third proofs returned to Publications Dept

10   Third proofs checked by editor and returned to designer

11   Any final corrections implemented by designer

12   Artwork sent on disk to printer

These steps can be presented in the form of a flowchart, as shown on page 12.

Flowchart of the
ideal process for
producing the
charity newsletter

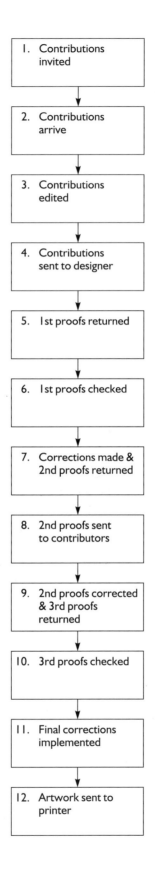

1. Contributions
   invited

2. Contributions
   arrive

3. Contributions
   edited

4. Contributions
   sent to designer

5. 1st proofs returned

6. 1st proofs checked

7. Corrections made &
   2nd proofs returned

8. 2nd proofs sent
   to contributors

9. 2nd proofs corrected
   & 3rd proofs
   returned

10. 3rd proofs checked

11. Final corrections
    implemented

12. Artwork sent to
    printer

This, of course, is a picture of the ideal process. What happens in reality is rather different.

Activity 7 · 5 mins

Have a look at the flowchart and jot down some ways in which you think each step might go wrong.

_____

_____

_____

_____

_____

_____

You could produce a very long list of ways in which each step might go wrong. To name just some of them: for step 2, some contributions might arrive late, they might be badly written, too short or too long, have no suggestions for pictures, or be accompanied by low-quality photographs. For step 3 it might prove difficult to get hold of or take the requested pictures. For step 4 it might only be possible to send some of the text and pictures to the designer. For step 5 the proofs might be incomplete or late. And so on.

All the things that can go wrong can be graphically illustrated in a flowchart, like the one on page 14, which shows the process as it actually happens.

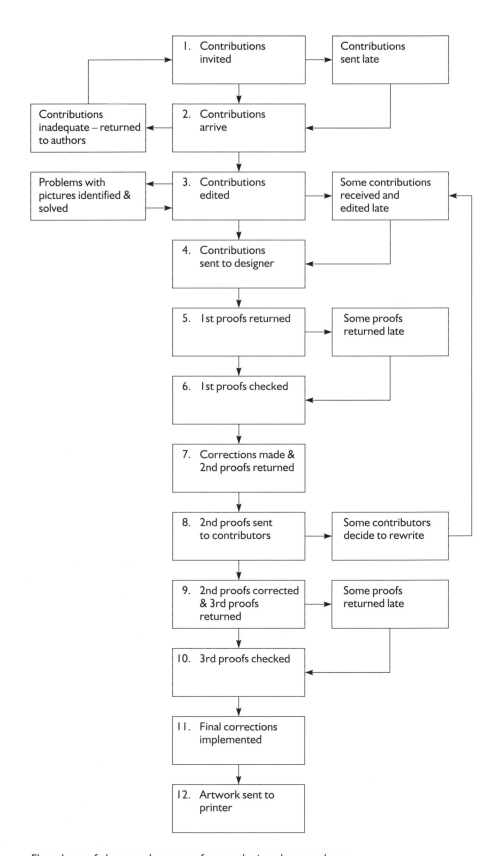

Flowchart of the actual process for producing the newsletter

Activity 8

20 mins

S/NVQ A1.3

This Activity may provide the basis of appropriate evidence for your S/NVQ portfolio. If you are intending to take this course of action, it might be better to write your answers on separate sheets of paper.

Return to Activity 4 and try drawing a flowchart of the process you chose in its ideal form. Then go through each step and list the various things that can go wrong. (You may want to try drawing a flowchart of the actual process, but this would take you more time than has been suggested for this Activity.)

At what steps in the process do you think changes could be made so that it is more likely to follow the ideal path? Note down a few ideas.

_____

_____

_____

_____

_____

_____

It's quite possible that doing this Activity will not have totally convinced you of the usefulness of flowcharting. It will at least partly depend on the complexity of the process you chose – if it only consists of a few steps you might well feel that you could manage perfectly well without it. However, you will find that when applied to a process made up of many steps in which there are lots of opportunities for things to go wrong, it can be very useful indeed.

3.3 Cause and effect diagrams

A cause and effect diagram is another tool for analysing processes. You will see its benefit as soon as you start to analyse processes in detail. Sometimes called a fishbone diagram because of its shape (or an 'Ishikawa' diagram after the person who devised it, Kaoru Ishikawa), it consists of a large arrow, into which smaller arrows lead. The large arrow represents a process or problem in a process. Each of the smaller arrows represents one of the main categories of inputs into the process, or possible causes of the problem. The categories will depend on the particular process you are looking at, but typical ones are:

- method (procedures);
- environment (physical conditions);
- personnel;
- equipment;
- materials;
- information or communication.

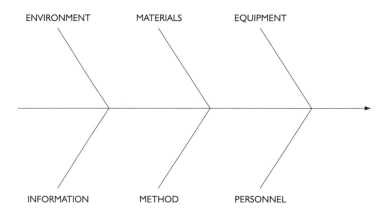

Typical categories in a cause and effect diagram

Activity 9

5 mins

Here are the beginnings of a cause and effect diagram for the process of producing the charity newsletter. What items would you add to each of the small arrows to make it more complete? Try to identify at least three and add them to the diagram.

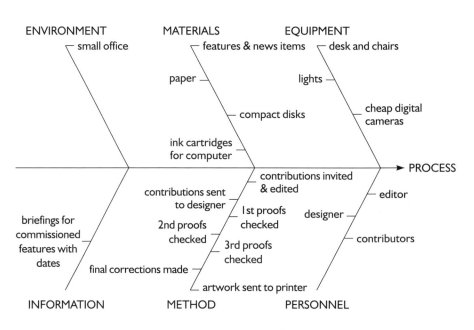

Among the most essential items missing from the diagram are the desks right next to each other (under environment); the Publications Officer (under personnel); a computer with modem (under equipment); an initial email calling for contributions (under information). You may well have thought of others.

If you take another look at the completed diagram, you can go through all the items and put a circle round anything you think presents an opportunity for improvement – as in the case of the features (their quality and late arrival) or the cheap digital camera.

You can see how this might be a useful tool for identifying possible improvements if you draw one that's relevant to your own situation.

Activity 10

15 mins

S/NVQ A1.3

This Activity may provide the basis of appropriate evidence for your S/NVQ portfolio. If you are intending to take this course of action, it might be better to write your answers on separate sheets of paper.

Return one final time to the process you first identified in Activity 4 and try drawing a cause and effect diagram for it in the space below.

Looking at the various items in your diagram, can you now add to the list of possible improvements that you drew up in Activity 4? Jot down any new ideas you have.

_____

_____

_____

4 The 5S Programme

As you will have gathered by now, if continuous improvement is to happen in an organization, everyone must get involved and take responsibility for it. One way of helping this process along is to introduce a 5S programme. Originating in Japan and first used in the UK by Japanese manufacturing companies – both on the shopfloor and in the office – it is now being adopted by other types of organization, such as construction companies.

The five 'S's are five Japanese words which few English speakers understand, so they are usually replaced with five English words beginning with S, such as:

- Sort
- Set in order
- Shine
- Standardize
- Sustain

Sometimes a sixth S – Safety – is added.

Some organizations prefer to use alternative versions of 5S, such as CANDO. This stands for:

- Cleanup
- Arranging
- Neatness
- Discipline
- Ongoing improvement

When you first look at these words you might think that 5S is all about good housekeeping. But it's actually a lot more than this, its aim being to create and maintain standardized and orderly operations.

4.1 The five steps of 5S

To get an idea of what each of the five steps entails, imagine a small, rather dingy metal-pressing factory. There are several large machines, all of which are dirty and covered with grease. On the floor, shoved into various corners, are boxes full of discarded materials. Various tools are strewn over the workbenches. In this situation, the staff often find it difficult to locate the tools they need. And when a machine breaks down it's often a big undertaking to find out where the problem lies. There's generally a feeling that things are a little chaotic and no one is surprised when the factory is late in getting an order out of the door.

In this situation, Step 1 of 5S, **Sort**, is about getting rid of everything that's not needed. The boxes of discarded materials can go for a start. Step 2, **Set in order**, means finding a place for everything that is needed. Where, for example, will all the tools go? Can workbenches be constructed where there is a clearly defined space for each one? Can more thought be given to the storage areas so that everyone knows exactly where to find stocks of particular materials and it's easy to spot when they are running out? Set in order also means ensuring that there is easy access to all areas and that the lighting is good.

Next comes Step 3, **Shine**, which is the job of making everything clean and tidy – and keeping it that way. When staff in the metal-pressing factory inspect the machines carefully they find all kinds of things that need to be taken care of, such as fittings caked with dirt, leaks of oil, and bolts loose or missing. There's also a fair amount of litter lying around the machines and workbenches that needs to be cleared away.

If the first three steps have been completed properly, everything should be ship-shape. But what next? How are the staff going to prevent the situation returning to what it was? Part of the answer is Step 4: **Standardize**. This means establishing and agreeing standards, and setting up systems for such things as the storing and handling of materials and getting rid of waste. It also means getting everyone into the habit of cleaning up throughout the day. (We will be returning to the subject of standards in the next section.)

Finally, there is Step 5: **Sustain**. This is about not only maintaining standards, but raising them. The key to doing this is to carry out a regular audit, at least once a week, of all physical aspects of the workplace, from walls, floors and walkways, to work benches, equipment and lighting. The audit is a fundamental part of any 5S programme, having a key role to play in the cycle of continuous improvement. It will reveal all the areas in which improvements could be made, ranging from small ones – such as the provision of more rubbish bins – to what might develop into major change projects, such as revising the layout of the factory.

Activity 11

5 mins

Imagine you work in an office where a 5S programme is introduced. What kinds of things do you think might be done in each of the first three steps?

_____

_____

_____

_____

_____

_____

Most offices have unnecessary piles of paper – either scattered around on work surfaces or shoved into filing cabinets – all of which need to be sorted out and the unnecessary items discarded. The same can be said for computer desktops. There's also often a need to set everything in order by getting proper filing systems established – both for paperwork and for computer files. How many people have had the experience of not being able to find the document they need at a particular moment? Dirt may not be as much of a problem in offices as it is in some factories, but untidiness often is. 'Shining' is all about such things as not leaving piles of paper clips or rubber bands lying around, regularly clearing away the empty tea or coffee cups, and generally keeping the desktop free of unnecessary papers. Having a tidy, orderly office environment helps many people to think more clearly and work in a methodical way.

Activity 12

Consider your own working environment. Jot down any ideas you have about the things that need to be done to:

- Sort it out
- Set things in order
- Make it 'shine'?

_____

_____

_____

_____

_____

_____

4.2 Visual management

You can help yourself and other people to maintain an orderly workplace – whether it's an office, factory, construction site or almost any other type of working environment – by using what is known as visual management. This involves using visually stimulating items, such as signs, lights, notice boards, and brightly or contrasting painted equipment, to catch people's attention and communicate important information.

The general rule is: 'The simpler, the better.'

In a factory or workshop setting, one simple example of visual management is the use of a shadow board. This is a board on which the shapes of various tools are painted, so that you only need to glance at it to see which tools are not in their allotted places. A similar device in an office is a piece of coloured tape run diagonally across the spines of a number of binders containing documents. Again, you only have to glance at the binders on the shelf to see a break in the line when a binder is not where it should be.

Another simple visual signal that is used in factory 5S programmes is the red tag. Suppose that someone carrying out an audit notices that equipment, materials or components have been left lying around, or that an item is dirty, defective or missing. The easiest way to alert people to the fact that there is a problem is to attach a red tag to the offending item, or the place where the item should be. The tag then stays there until corrective action has been taken.

Activity 13

5 mins

Notice boards can be an excellent way of passing on information and letting people know about what progress is being made in a 5S or any other type of programme. In fact, notice boards are among the items included in 5S audits. Some typical questions about them are listed overleaf. Try answering them in relation to your own workplace, making suggestions for improvements in the Comments column.

Noticeboards: key points	Yes	No	Comment
Are they positioned so that everyone has easy access to at least one?			
Is the display free of clutter and easy to read?			
Are the items on the boards relevant and up-to-date?			
Are the items well-designed, with easy-to-read text and eye-catching pictures?			
Other			

Visual management will help you to maintain a working environment that is orderly – and so more productive – on a continuous basis. So, too, will the setting of standards. In fact, setting standards is one of the keys to continuous improvement.

5 Standards and continuous improvement

Think of your last visit to the dentist. Did you have to wait long to check in at reception – and was the receptionist who checked you in friendly or off-hand? Did you have to sit in a waiting room that had several comfortable chairs, was well-lit, had a variety of recent magazines for you to read, and even had a few toys for small children to play with? Or did you have to wait in a small, dingy room with uncomfortable chairs and a pile of ancient magazines? Were you told that the dentist was ready to see you almost immediately, or did you have to wait an awfully long time as the sound of drilling came down the corridor?

Then, when you actually got into the dentist's room, did you feel it was a pleasant space in which you could feel reasonably relaxed – or exactly the opposite? Did you find your dentist pleasant, and the check-up and treatment relatively painless? Or did you dislike everything to do with the experience, from the way the dentist spoke to you to the way he or she dealt with your teeth?

And what about the actual treatment? Was the filling, for example, satisfactory, or did it feel a bit rough, with part of it breaking off a couple of months after it was done? Did the price of the treatment strike you as incredibly high or perfectly reasonable?

These questions have asked you about three different aspects of the service. These are:

- the structure – that is, the physical and organizational framework within which the service was given, such as the waiting room, the dentist's room, and the arrangements for checking in;
- the process – that is, the way you were treated on a personal level by the various members of staff, and the procedures followed by the dentist and his or her assistant in deciding what, if any, treatment you needed, and then delivering the treatment;
- the outcome – that is, the effect of the treatment plus its costs.

Any dentist who wants a flourishing practice will aim to provide a quality service – and this will mean drawing up standards for all three aspects. However, if the practice is to continue to flourish in the future, this will not be enough. The service will need to improve on a continuous basis, which means that once a standard has been met, a new standard will have to be drawn up.

The diagram shows this relationship between standard-setting and continuous improvement.

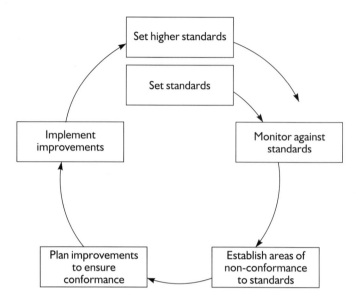

Relationship
between continuous
improvement and
standards

5.1 Setting standards

The relationship between standards and continuous improvement always exists, no matter whether the standards apply to a service or a product. Let's return to the example of the metal-pressing factory to see what this might mean in practice.

Structure

A 5S audit is carried out in the factory at the end of the day twice a week. Each time the auditor finds that tools have been left lying around in a haphazard fashion on workbenches and haven't been returned to their correct positions. A suitable standard might be:

> All tools to be returned to their correct positions by the end of each day.

This standard is not reached straight away. It takes a while for people to get into the habit of always spending a few minutes at the end of the day making sure that all their tools are in the correct place. However, once it has been reached, it's time to consider a standard aimed at further improvement, such as:

> All tools to be returned to their correct positions whenever they are not in use.

Process

One of the processes in the factory involves pressing and cutting the metal clasps on car seat belts. Sometimes there are hold-ups in the process because the press operator runs out of sheets of metal to cut and press. And the reason for this is that the staff in stores have not sorted out deliveries of materials efficiently enough. An appropriate standard for the stores department might be that:

> All deliveries of materials to be unpacked and put in the correct place within 45 minutes of arrival on site.

Once this has been achieved, perhaps the time of 45 minutes can be reduced to 30.

Outcome

Before the metal seat belt clasps are sent out of the factory to be coated with chrome, a random check is carried out to make sure they are conforming to the specification. Unfortunately, it appears that an average of six in every hundred has some kind of defect. A suitable standard to aim for in this situation would be:

> Number of defects in metal clasps not to exceed an average of two per hundred.

Then, once this standard has been achieved, the factory can aim for no defects at all as part of a cycle of continuous improvement.

Activity 14 · 3 mins

Have another look at the various standards suggested for the metal pressing factory. Is there anything they all have in common?

One obvious thing the standards all have in common is that it's easy to see how they can be upgraded as part of the drive to achieve continuous improvement. Perhaps not so obvious is the fact that they are all unambiguous. Standards that are ambiguous are not useful. Suppose, for example, that one of the standards was:

All deliveries of materials to be unpacked and put in the correct place as quickly as possible.

How would you know when the standard had been met? The term 'as quickly as possible' can mean different things to different people and so cannot serve the function of giving everyone in the Stores Department a definite goal to achieve.

As well as being unambiguous, standards should also be realistic and achievable. It's no good setting standards that people have no chance of achieving with the available resources. The manager of the Stores Department, for example, should not set the standard 'All deliveries of materials to be unpacked and put in the correct place within 45 minutes of arrival on site' if he does not have enough staff to make this possible. If it's inevitable that staff will inevitably fail to meet a standard, they will end up being demotivated.

This brings us to another point about setting standards. It will not be easy to get staff to feel motivated about changing their working practices to meet a standard if they have not been involved in setting it. You should always consult with your team when drawing up standards.

Activity 15

S/NVQ A1.3

This Activity may provide the basis of appropriate evidence for your S/NVQ portfolio. If you are intending to take this course of action, it might be better to write your answers on separate sheets of paper.

Pick out one area of work for which you are responsible and try writing a standard, if possible with another member of staff, that:

You will need your answer to this Activity for Activity 16.

■ represents an improvement in a work process or its outcome;
■ is unambiguous;
■ is achievable within the available resources.

5.2 Monitoring standards

As you've already seen, if standards are to form part of the cycle of continuous improvement, they must be monitored to discover whether they are being met. If they are not, then you will need to consider why, and plan how to ensure they are met in the future.

Use of audits

Exactly what method you use to monitor a standard will depend on what type of standard it is. Standards concerned with 'structure' – that is, the physical and organizational framework within which people work – can be monitored through auditing, as in a 5S programme. Take, for example, the standard:

All tools to be returned to their correct positions when not in use.

It's easy to see how you could include a relevant question on an audit form, to which the answer is Yes or No. You might even be able to assess the extent to which the standard is being met on a scale of 1 to 5 and make a comment on what more needs to be done.

AUDIT FORM

1 Tools and equipment	Yes	No	Extent of non-compliance/ compliance on scale of 1–5	Comment
Are all tools in correct positions when not in use?				

Other methods

Standards for processes and outcomes in manufacturing, where there is something tangible to be recorded – such as the number of defects in a week – are comparatively straightforward to monitor. The relevant data is collected and recorded in graphs which immediately show where there are problems.

Standards relating to the way a service is delivered are more difficult. Take the standard:

All customers should be made to feel welcome.

There is nothing that can be measured and recorded in a graph. One alternative is to ask customers for their views on whether the standard is being achieved, and then record their views in a table like the one below.

	Achieved	Partially achieved	Not achieved	What needs to be done
All customers made to feel welcome				

How the relevant information is gathered will depend on your particular situation. You can ask staff, customers, or both, to complete forms and questionnaires. You can ask staff to generally monitor their own performance, but also carry out some spot checks yourself. And in an organization committed to achieving quality, you can establish a quality circle and get them to monitor standards.

Activity 16

5 mins

S/NVQ A1.1

Have a look at the standard you wrote for Activity 15. What method could you use for monitoring this standard and gathering the necessary information?

_____

_____

_____

_____

Monitoring standards will inevitably indicate areas where improvements can be made. Remember: standards are key to achieving change on a continuous basis.

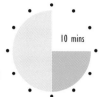

Self-assessment 1

10 mins

For questions 1 to 5 complete the sentences with a suitable word or words from the following list:

CONDITIONS PROCESSES CAUSE
NEEDS   RESOURCES FISHBONE DIAGRAM
PROCEDURES FLOWCHART STEPS

1 At the heart of continuous improvement is the idea that if customers' constantly changing _____ and wants are to be met, improvements must be made to _____ – and consequently products and services – in small _____, at all levels, forever.

2 You and your staff may have ideas for improvements regarding the physical _____ in which you work, the _____ you work with, your relationships with other people within and outside the organization, and the _____ you and your staff follow.

3 A useful tool for mapping out the steps in a process is a _____.

4 A useful tool for mapping out all the inputs to a process is a _____.

5 'Five Whys' is a useful technique for getting to the root _____ of a particular outcome or effect.

6 Which of the following do the 5 Ss stand for?
 a Sort, Streamline, Shine, Set in order and Sustain.
 b Sort, Set in order, Shine, Standardize and Sustain
 c Sort, Streamline, Shine, Standardize and Sustain
 d Sort, Set in order, Streamline, Standardize and Sustain

7 Which of the following statements about 5S are TRUE and which are FALSE?
 a Sorting is about finding a place for everything. TRUE/FALSE
 b Setting in order is about arranging everything in neat piles. TRUE/FALSE
 c Standardizing is about establishing standards and setting up systems for such things as storing and handling materials and getting rid of waste. TRUE/FALSE
 d Sustaining is all about maintaining standards. TRUE/FALSE

8   Can you complete this diagram illustrating the role of standards in continuous improvement by filling in the gap at the top?

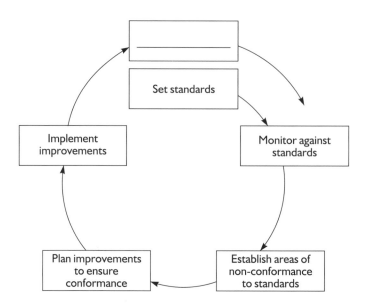

9   What process can play an important part in the monitoring of some standards as well as in a 5S programme?

_____

Answers to these questions can be found on pages 96–7.

6 Summary

- Continuous improvement means continuously improving processes – and consequently products and services – in order to meet and then exceed customers' expectations.

- The benefits of continuous improvement were first recognized in Japan, where it is referred to as *kaizen*.

- As a manager you have a vital role to play in identifying ways in which processes can be improved, and encouraging your staff to do so.

- Improvements may be to do with:
  - the physical conditions in which you and your staff work;
  - the resources you and your staff work with;
  - the relationships you have with other people, both within and outside the organization;
  - the procedures you and your staff follow.

- Tools and techniques for aiding continuous improvement include:
  - 'Five Whys';
  - process flowcharting;
  - fishbone or cause and effect diagrams;
  - 5S programmes;
  - visual management.

- The 5 Ss are five Japanese words. One English-language version of the 5 Ss is:
  - Sort;
  - Set in order;
  - Shine;
  - Standardize;
  - Sustain.

- Fundamental to all 5S programmes is the process of auditing the workplace.

- Essential to continuous improvement is the setting and monitoring of standards.

- Standards can relate to:
  - structure – that is, the physical and organizational framework within which a service is provided or a product manufactured;
  - process – that is, the procedures employed in providing the service or manufacturing the product, and the way in which they are employed;
  - outcome – that is, the quality of the actual product or the effect of the service.

Session B
Planning change

1 Introduction

So far in this workbook we have looked at what's involved in gradual change that takes place over a period of time. More specifically, we have looked at what's involved in making small changes to improve the quality of processes, products and services on a continuous basis.

In this session we are going to switch focus and concentrate on a second form of change: major and dramatic change. Such change has to be planned very carefully if it is to be successful. As a first line manager you have an important part to play in this process, ensuring that objectives are set, actions to achieve these objectives are identified and assigned to the most appropriate members of staff, and that results are monitored against the objectives.

We will be examining this planning process in some detail. But first we are going to consider the nature of major change and the reasons for it.

2 Reasons for major change

Activity 17 · 5 mins

Think back over your own working life and/or that of other members of your family or friends. What major changes have occurred in the organizations you or they have worked for? Jot down two or three.

_____

_____

_____

In almost any organization there's a good chance that major change has taken place in recent years in one or more of the following ways:

■ the development of a totally new product or service;
■ a significant expansion or reduction of the workforce;
■ a merger with, or a take-over of/by another organization;
■ restructuring to eliminate layers of management and/or create new departmental boundaries;
■ the relocation of premises.

The ultimate aim of any commercial organization in making such a major change is to increase its profits. But the precise nature of the change will depend on a number of factors, both within and outside the organization. As in the case of small-scale gradual change, internal factors include the need for improvements in physical conditions, resources (including finance), staff skills, relationships and procedures. Factors within the external environment may be of a political, economic, social, technological, legal or environmental nature.

■ **Political factors**
The nature of the government and the policies it pursues can have a major impact on organizations. Just one example is the introduction in 2001 of the Climate Change Levy, a tax on businesses which is designed to encourage

them to reduce their energy consumption. Such a tax reflects the government's growing concern over the need to reduce the consumption of finite resources, and it means that manufacturers, in particular, need to find ways of using energy more efficiently.

■ Economic factors

Some developments in the economy are dictated by government policies, notably measures announced in the annual budget. Others are outside the government's control. The discovery in 2002, for example, that large American corporations such as Enron and WorldCom had claimed to have made huge profits when in fact they had made none, led to a dramatic drop in the value of almost all organizations' shares on both the American and UK stock markets.

■ Social factors

Among the long-term social factors that have had a major impact in recent years is the ageing of the population coupled with the growing power of the youth market. Among the more short-term social factors are changing fashions in such things as clothes and food.

■ Technological factors

Personal computers, mobile phones and the Internet – all are among the numerous technological developments that have created big changes in people's lives, and in the way organizations function, as well as in the goods and services they offer.

■ Legal factors

Laws and regulations, whether they be at local, national or European level, affect organizations in numerous ways. They range from measures to protect employees and consumers to measures aimed at controlling all aspects of an organization's activities. Just one simple example is a planned European regulation for scrapped cars to be returned to the manufacturers, thus putting pressure on them to produce cars whose parts can be recycled.

■ Environmental factors

The planned European regulation on cars is a reflection of the growing concern with environmental factors. These fall into two categories:

- those concerning pollution of the Earth and its atmosphere by all forms of waste, ranging from gases to oil rigs;
- those concerning the over-exploitation of the Earth's finite resources.

Concern over environmental factors has resulted in many laws and regulations that affect the activities of organizations. It has also created many opportunities for organizations, such as The Body Shop and its competitors, to develop new products for consumers who wish to purchase goods that use natural, replaceable resources and recyclable packaging.

All the various types of factor discussed above can represent both threats and opportunities to an organization. Either way, any organization that chooses to ignore them, and not change, will lose out in the end. (You can read more about the various forces for change in another workbook in this series entitled *Understanding Change*.)

3 Change and the first line manager

Major changes at work do not simply happen: they are made to work by people. The job of managers is to give the lead to their teams. This does not mean that people have to be told exactly what to do and when and how to do it. The primary skill of leading and managing is to find ways of gaining:

- influence;
- trust and respect;
- voluntary co-operation;
- commitment to the task.

First line managers are very often put under pressure before anyone else by senior management's requirements for change. Higher management may make plans for the organization as a whole, but more often than not it is the first line manager who has to turn these plans into reality.

Activity 18

S/NVQ A1.1

This Activity may provide the basis of appropriate evidence for your S/NVQ portfolio. If you are intending to take this course of action, it might be better to write your answers on separate sheets of paper.

Before we continue this session, think about your own work situation, and if possible identify two fairly major changes, one which you have already experienced, and one which you expect could happen in the near future.

In each case, briefly describe the change.

a What was the event that has already taken place? What contribution did you and your team make to it?

_____

_____

_____

_____

_____

_____

_____

_____

_____

_____

_____

_____

b What is the change that you expect to be involved in shortly? Explain how you and your team plan to play your part in its implementation.

_____

_____

_____

_____

_____

_____

_____

_____

_____

_____

You will need your answer to Activity 18a for Activities 19, 20, 21, 30, 32 and 36. You will need your answer to Activity 18b for Activities 23, 25, 26 and 31.

3.1 The first line manager as an instigator of change

In many organizations, plans for change that will affect more than one team are instigated by the higher levels of management. However, this need not always be the case, as the following example illustrates.

On a construction site for a complex of large buildings, Michael was manager of the wall-building team. One of the things about his job that had often annoyed him in the past was that the team who installed the ducting, through which the wiring passed in the ceiling area, always worked ahead of his team. This meant that when his team came to build a wall, they had to spend at least half a day making fine adjustments to its design, and then implementing these adjustments, to take account of where the ducting was positioned. This often meant working for a long time on a ladder supported by scaffolding, with your head back. This was not only uncomfortable but an incredible waste of time. Michael thought there had to be a better way of doing this and decided to talk to the site planner, who was responsible for sorting out the sequencing of work. The site planner agreed he had a point and suggested that a meeting be arranged which was to be attended by herself, Michael, the manager of the ducting team, and at least one building designer.

It quickly became apparent during this meeting that the designers did not always know exactly where the interior walls were going to go once the outer shell of the building had been constructed. Sometimes this outer shell had been erected just a few centimetres to the side of its planned position, but this did not mean that the designers then recalculated the positions of the interior walls. Neither they nor the planner had any idea of the importance for the teams doing the actual construction of knowing the exact position of the interface between the ducting and walls.

After much discussion and drawing of alternative process flowcharts on a whiteboard, it was agreed that in future the main stages of the process for installing walls and ducting should be as follows:

1 Once shell is in place, designer to establish whether it accords exactly with drawings and make any necessary amendments to drawings.
2 Designer to mark out on floor exactly where walls should go.
3 Plumb lines to be dropped from ceiling to exact points on floor where walls are to go, thus locating exact position of interfaces between walls and ducting.
4 Work on construction of walls to proceed before ducting is installed. Once a wall is approaching ceiling area, members of walling team to take a piece of rectangular ducting and install it within top of wall.
5 Once all interfaces between walls and length of ducting have been constructed, ducting team to install remainder of ducting.

When the various people involved in this process tried it out over the course of the next few weeks, they found that the job of installing a piece of ducting in the top of a wall took about 30 minutes. This compared exceedingly well with the half-day it had previously taken for the walling team to do the best they could with the ducting that was already in place. In a building with six walls this represented a saving in time of at least 18 hours – which in turn represented a big financial saving for the construction company.

In this example, just one small idea for change had important implications for a number of different people and the organization they worked for. In looking for ways of improving processes, products and services, you too may come up with ideas that have important implications for your organization and require you to work with other managers. Why not seize the initiative and voice your ideas to your manager? You may need permission to put the change into effect, but your idea and enterprise will almost certainly stand you in good stead.

Activity 19

3 mins

S/NVQ A1.1

Take a look at your description of a change in Activity 18a. Was it one that you helped to instigate, or was it imposed on you by senior management? Whatever your answer, what do you think was the main reason for the change? Was it, for example, made in response to economic factors in the external environment, or in response to something within the organization, such as the inefficient use of resources?

_____

_____

_____

_____

Whether or not external forces for change played a part in prompting the change you have described, you should bear in mind that as a manager you should always be aware of such forces – be they economic, social, technological, political, legal or environmental.

3.2 Other elements in the first line manager's role

As well as instigating change, your role as a first line manager in change will encompass:

■ **calculating costs**
You may simply be presented with a budget to manage. Alternatively, you may be asked to estimate costs of particular actions or processes.

■ **determining feasibility**
You and your fellow first line managers are often in the best position to know whether a proposal will work, or is achievable within a certain timescale or cost limit.

■ **feeding back information**
Your experience and your team may be key to the project, and you will be expected to contribute information to support the decisions made by your line managers and others.

Activity 20

S/NVQ C12.3

This Activity may provide the basis of appropriate evidence for your S/NVQ portfolio. If you are intending to take this course of action, it might be better to write your answers on separate sheets of paper.

Looking back at the change in Activity 18a, describe how you gave feedback to your team which resulted in a modification to a planned change. Alternatively, choose another occasion when you gave feedback to your team, which resulted in the modification of plans.

_____

_____

_____

_____

_____

_____

_____

_____

_____

_____

Other elements in your role as leader of change may include:

■ **working out a strategy for deployment of staff**
Staff deployment is usually part of the first line manager's day-to-day job. Where substantial changes are underway, this aspect of the work can become more difficult than usual.

■ **'selling' the idea of change to the team**
To sell something, whether it is a product, a process or an idea, it is necessary to persuade potential buyers that they will benefit from the exchange. In this case, the workteam will pay you in their commitment to the project.

■ **empowering the workteam to cope with the change**
It is not enough to sell the idea. You must empower your workteam to manage things in their own way. More and more, organizations are realizing that the old ways of managing by telling people what to do and how to do it are no longer appropriate. As competition gets more fierce, greater commitment is needed from staff at all levels. The only way to achieve this is by allowing increased levels of freedom for people to organize their own work – to hand over control of tasks to those who have to accomplish them.

Handing over more authority to your team is a courageous step. It involves watching them learn from their mistakes. It cannot be taken lightly. If and when you do it, the workteam will certainly depend on your full trust and support.

You will also have to provide them with the practical resources and training they need beforehand.

Activity 21 · 10 mins

Portfolio of evidence

S/NVQ C12.1, B1.1

This Activity may provide the basis of appropriate evidence for your S/NVQ portfolio. If you are intending to take this course of action, it might be better to write your answers on separate sheets of paper.

For the project you described in Activity 18a, describe the recommendations you made, and the steps you took, to provide the workteam with the necessary resources, (perhaps) including training.

_____

_____

_____

_____

_____

Continuing our discussion of your role as leader of change, your tasks should include:

■ **providing your team with the feeling of ownership of the change**
Once you have sold the idea of the change, you can complete the deal by handing over the ownership. Your team will be a lot more committed to the change if they feel they are controlling the action themselves and are:

- not being kept in the dark;
- not simply looking on from the sidelines;
- not just helping implement the plans of management.

If you can manage to do this, they will become enthusiastic about the change, and promote it to others.

■ **keeping the team informed**
It is essential that you keep the team informed throughout all stages of the change process, from the time you announce the change to your final evaluation of what the change has achieved. You'll find more on this subject in the next section.

■ **coping with keeping things running during the change**
This may be your greatest challenge.

3.3 Keeping the team informed

In implementing change, the keys to success include empowering your team to cope with the change and giving them a sense of ownership, thus ensuring their full **participation** in the change process. Another key to success is ensuring that your team always receives sufficient **information**. Finally, there is the need for you to inspire **enthusiasm** by being enthusiastic yourself whenever possible. This is the PIE recipe, which is discussed in more detail in *Understanding Change*. Here we are going to focus on the importance of keeping your team informed right from the beginning of any change programme.

Activity 22

5 mins

At the HiPrint works, there was a lot of discussion going on. It was a well-known fact that the company had been looking for new premises for some time. A few months previously, a lot of the staff had expressed concern that the company would move away from the town – perhaps to one of those remote government development areas – and that everyone would be given the choice of moving house or finding a new job. But nothing seemed to come of the idea and the workforce more or less forgot about it.

Now the rumour was going around that a new site had been found, five miles on the other side of town. As you can imagine, a lot of questions were being asked.

What do you think the main concerns of the workforce would be? Write down **three** or **four** questions that might be going through their minds.

_____

_____

_____

_____

_____

_____

They would probably be asking questions like:

'Will any of us lose our jobs through the move – perhaps they'll try to recruit people in the local area?'

'How will I get to work? Is there a bus service? Will the company provide a company bus?'

'Will it mean that we'll have to get up earlier, or get home later?'

'Will we be paid compensation?'

'Will it be more – or less – pleasant to work in?'

'If there are bigger premises, will there now be room for a canteen?'

In short, every member of the workforce will want to know:

'How will the change affect me? Will it bring new problems and how will I deal with them? Will it perhaps bring new opportunities?'

If you've ever been involved in a major change like moving premises, you will know something of the headaches it brings. For the first line manager, it can mean a hundred new problems, often compounded by the fact that management insist on minimum work being lost during the move.

For the team member, the worries are more personal. The greatest fear in any upheaval is job loss. After that, the concern will be over money, disturbance, intrusion and inconvenience. These anxieties are in addition to the unease felt about changes related to the job itself. The effects of all these cares may be to cause:

■ emotional outbursts;
■ unreasonable and unreasoning behaviour;
■ lowering of work performance;
■ sickness or other absence;
■ argument and other conflict.

Once all the uncertainty has been resolved, most of the worries disappear and the mood changes – even before the change takes place.

It isn't change that creates the anxiety so much as uncertainty about change. And to avoid uncertainty, you need to provide information.

4 Preparing for change

The period in which you prepare people for change is often referred to as the 'unfreezing' stage. Of course, you can't embark on this until you yourself know what form the change is going to take. There is nothing more likely to cause mounting levels of anxiety than making an announcement that there is going to be change and then not saying anything more about it. So the first thing you need to do in any major change is to define its scope – that is, produce a broad outline of what it will involve.

4.1 Defining the scope of change

When considering a major change, it is useful to think of it as a project, or even as a number of projects. Doing this will help you to define the scope of the change, as in the following example.

> Stella was the manager of a long-established health club which was beginning to lose clients to a new club that had opened up a couple of miles away. From talking to the reception staff about various comments made by clients, she knew there had been several causes for complaint, including:
>
> - changing and shower facilities not always as clean as they might be;
> - pieces of equipment in the gym often faulty or broken down completely;
> - general lack of interest among staff in client progress with exercise regimes in the gym;
> - bottlenecks for various items of apparatus at most popular times;
> - reception and café areas not very inviting;
> - insufficient number of yoga classes;
> - teachers not always turning up for their classes.
>
> Clearly a major overhaul of the club was necessary if it was to stop losing clients and attract new ones. It was going to require some investment from the owners, training for the staff in the fundamentals of client care, and some reorganization of the way various things –

such as the cleaning and maintenance of the equipment in the gym – were done. And once all the improvements had been made they would have to be publicized in order to attract new clients.

It was a lot of work for one person to manage while still keeping the club running as efficiently as possible on a day-to-day basis. Stella decided that the only way to handle it was to think of the work as five sub-projects and delegate responsibility for them to five sub-teams:

■ redesigning the reception area and café;
■ getting procedures and rotas for general maintenance and cleaning sorted out;
■ establishing what classes should be run when, and identifying possible teachers;
■ sorting out how the gym was run;
■ organizing and distributing a publicity brochure.

Having got this far, Stella was well on the way to defining the project's scope and putting this in the form of a proposal to the club's owner. But first she needed to establish:

■ who was going to be in the project team (or sub-teams);
■ the project's aims and objectives;
■ the approximate timescale and budget.

For Stella, deciding who was going to be in the team was easy: it had to be her whole team, which was all 12 full-time members of staff. She hoped that involving everyone in this way would actually be a first step to getting them more committed to the club and more prepared to look after the clients properly. However, drawing up the list of aims and objectives, and working out the approximate timescale and budget, was more problematic. She didn't think that she yet had sufficient information to do this properly. She would have to hold some meetings with her team, and possibly collect more data on what clients actually wanted, before she could complete her proposal.

Activity 23

5 mins

S/NVQ C12.1

This Activity may provide the basis of appropriate evidence for your S/NVQ portfolio. If you are intending to take this course of action, it might be better to write your answers on separate sheets of paper.

Look back at the change you described in Activity 18b. How would you define its scope? Is it possible to think of it as a number of sub-projects? If so, what are they?

_____

_____

_____

_____

4.2 Establishing aims and objectives

The importance of getting the objectives clear before the start of a change project can never be over-emphasized. If you don't know what you're aiming for, it's hard to achieve it. However, to be realistic, at the start of a project you may only be able to sketch out your main aims. You will then have to refine these at a later stage.

When producing your objectives you will find it helpful to bear in mind the SMART principle, which means that they are:

■ Specific – they state precisely what is to be achieved;
■ Measurable – their achievement is easy to assess;
■ Achievable – they can be attained given the current situation and the available skills and resources;
■ Relevant – they are of significance to the organization;
■ Time bound – the state precisely when something is to be achieved.

Activity 24 · 5 mins

Thinking back to Stella and the health club, she might have said that one of her broad aims was to improve the level of cleanliness in the changing and shower areas. Can you suggest how this might have been rephrased as a SMART objective?

_____

_____

_____

Of course, there are numerous possible answers to this question. The following objective is just one of them: 'Within one month, establish a system for regular checking that the changing and shower areas are clear of litter and dirt, and for ensuring that these areas are cleaned thoroughly at least twice a day.' This assumes that there are sufficient staff to carry out this amount of checking and cleaning. If there are not, then the objective is not achievable.

Whatever the objectives of the project, it is best to agree them with the people involved wherever possible. However, you shouldn't expect to stick rigidly to this rule. If management has instigated the change, the objectives may be defined already, although they may need to be modified in some way. And it may not be wise to get the team involved in setting objectives if the project is going to lead to redundancies. (We will return to the subject of redundancies in Session C.) You will have to make up your own mind about the most appropriate time at which to get your team involved, depending on the situation.

Activity 25 · 10 mins

S/NVQ C12.1

This Activity may provide the basis of appropriate evidence for your S/NVQ portfolio. If you are intending to take this course of action, it might be better to write your answers on separate sheets of paper.

Return to the change project you outlined in Activity 18b. Does the project have stated aims and objectives? If so, how might they be modified to take account of your team's particular circumstances or to make them more SMART? If there are not stated aims or objectives, what suggestions do you have on what they should be?

_____

_____

_____

_____

_____

_____

4.3 Establishing timescale and budget

At the outset of a change project it may only be possible to give a very approximate idea of the timescale and budget. And even when you have worked these out – or they've been worked out for you by senior management – it may, in fact, be necessary to carry out a feasibility study before you begin any serious planning.

The purpose of a feasibility study is to establish whether the desired outcomes of the project can be achieved within the available time and resources, most notably the budget and staff. When carrying out a feasibility study it is often very useful to include a cost-benefit analysis. This is discussed in some detail in the workbook entitled _Making a Financial Case_. In this workbook we will note simply that financial costs are often divided into two main categories:

■ development costs – that is, the costs of the actual project;
■ operational costs – that is, the running costs after the project has been completed.

Benefits are also often divided into two categories: financial and non-financial. In the case of Stella and the health club, for example, the intended main financial benefit of the change project is obviously increased revenue from an increasing number of clients. Non-financial benefits could include a more motivated staff, leading to improved quality of service, which in turn should help to increase the number of clients.

Activity 26 ·

10 mins

S/NVQ C12.1, B1.1

This Activity may provide the basis of appropriate evidence for your S/NVQ portfolio. If you are intending to take this course of action, it might be better to write your answers on separate sheets of paper.

Returning to the change project outlined in Activity 18b, consider the following questions:

a What is the proposed timescale?

Does the timescale appear reasonable? Is it feasible? If you don't think it is, what can you do about this?

_____

_____

b What are the financial constraints?

Do you have a budget for the part of the change project for which you are responsible? If so, do you think it is enough? If you don't think it's enough, do you at least have a rough idea of how much you need?

_____

_____

c Which people are available to help you in both the planning and implementation stages? And how much of their time will you require?

Is it the same group of people for both, or are there people who may be involved in one stage but not the other? Are there people, for example, from other teams or departments who need to be consulted in the planning stage but do not need to be involved in actual implementation?

_____

_____

d What other resources (apart from finance and people) do you need in both stages?

_____

_____

You may have found it very difficult to answer these questions. It's not until you begin the detailed planning of a project that you begin to see exactly how long it is likely to take, and how much staff time and other resources you will need.

In practice you are sometimes given a date by which a project has to be completed and you then have to work backwards from that in your planning, rather than the other way round. You may also have to plan around the staff who are available to help – and the number of hours they are able to devote to your project – rather than beginning with your ideal requirements.

5 Planning the project activities

Once you have established the aims and objectives of the change project you need to set about planning exactly how you are going to achieve them – that is, establishing the key project activities and the order in which they should be completed. If you have not been able to do so before, this is certainly the point at which you need to involve your team.

There are a number of tools you and your team may find very useful in planning the project activities. The main ones are:

- logic diagrams;
- critical path diagrams;
- Gantt charts.

5.1 Logic diagrams

Constructing a logic diagram will help you to identify the key stages in the project and the order in which they should occur. Begin by establishing with your team what the main activities in the project will be: first write everyone's ideas on a whiteboard or flipchart and then decide what the main activities actually are. You don't want to end up with an unmanageable number. You can then write each activity on a sticky-note or piece of adhesive coloured card and arrange these on the flipchart or board until you have them in a logical order. The final step is to draw the diagram with arrows between the stages.

To return to Stella and the health club. The additional data she collected on clients' wants revealed that in addition to more yoga classes, they also wanted classes in Pilates and the Alexander technique.

The clients also had a lot to say about how the gym was run. For a start, they didn't like the way there were bottlenecks for some pieces of equipment during peak times. But more fundamental was the feeling that no one on the staff took a personal interest in them once their initial exercise regime had been established at the beginning of the year.

Finally, there was the café. Not only did they want the décor to be improved, they also wanted a better selection of drinks and snacks.

Stella produced a proposal taking all the new data into account and she secured the go-ahead from the owner. During discussions of the proposal with the staff, it was decided that the main activities were as follows:

A   Draw up detailed proposals for redesign of reception area and café.
B   Consult with clients on their views about designs and amend accordingly.
C   Organize redecoration and installation of new furniture.
D   Consult with clients on drinks and snacks they want in café.
E   Organize deliveries of requested drinks and snacks.
F   Establish procedures for checking state of changing and shower facilities, and cleaning during day.
G   Draw up rota for checking and cleaning procedures.
H   Establish procedures for checking equipment in gym every day and arranging for any broken equipment to be repaired.
I   Draw up rota for checking equipment.
J   Draw up new list of classes.
K   Consult with clients on list of classes to establish best times plus level of demand.
L   Recruit teachers for classes.
M   Organize and run client care session for teachers to stress importance of turning up on time and being well-prepared.
N   Set up appointments system for gym during peak periods (lunchtimes and evenings).
O   Organize client care session for all non-teaching staff, with emphasis on how to look after clients in gym.
P   Run client care sessions.
Q   Establish system for ensuring that clients in gym receive personal attention from one staff member throughout the year.
R   Organize publicity brochure.
S   Distribute publicity brochure.

Activity 27

3 mins

In the list above:

- Which activities could be combined?

  _____

- Which activities should, ideally, be carried out first, in parallel with each other?

  _____

Activities B, D and K, all of which involve consulting with clients, could be carried out at the same time. So too, perhaps, could Activities M and O, both of which are concerned with giving staff training in client care.

Activities A, F, H, J, and N should all, ideally, be carried out first in parallel with each other. (R – Organize publicity brochure – is another possibility, but it's probably best to produce this after the consultation exercise has been completed.) Whether this is actually possible in practice will depend on the number of staff available. It would be no good getting so many staff involved in the change project at any one time that they couldn't continue with the day-to-day work of running the club at least to present standards.

In fact, Stella and her team decided that they could carry out A, F, H, J and N in parallel, and so ended up with the logic diagram on the next page.

There are a number of things to notice about this diagram:

- The diagram begins with 'Start' and ends with 'Finish'.
- The arrows show which activities are dependent on other activities.
- There is no timescale.
- No activities are assigned to people.

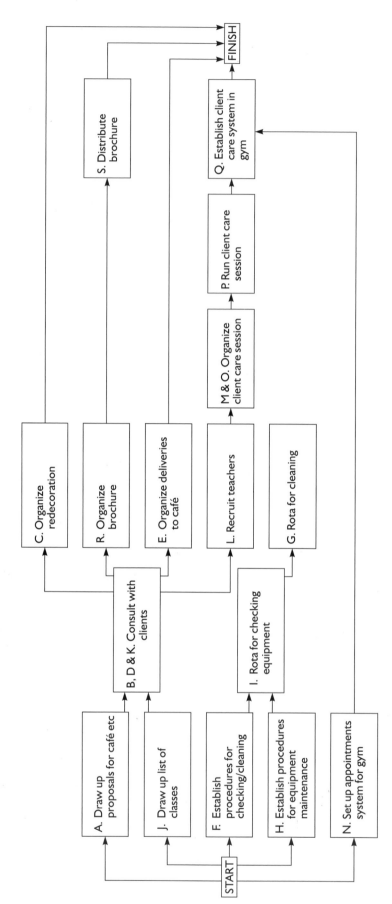

Logic diagram for health club change project

5.2 Critical path diagrams

A critical path diagram is a useful tool for estimating precisely the time a change project will take, and drawing up a schedule. A critical path diagram (also known as a network analysis) is a useful tool for doing this, as it shows how long individual activities should take and the relationship between them.

Let's first assume you haven't been given a completion date that you must achieve. The first step is to look at each of the main activities included in your logic diagram and decide with your team:

■ what the activity consists of and how long it will take;
■ which staff should carry it out:
■ given the existing workload of those staff, how many days/weeks/months it will take them to complete the activity.

Taking all these factors into account, here is Stella's list of estimated times for activities:

Key activity		Estimated time in weeks
A	Draw up proposals for redesign of reception area and café	2
B, D, K	Consult with clients	3
C	Organize redecoration and installation of new furniture	4
E	Organize deliveries of requested drinks and snacks	I
F	Establish checking and cleaning procedures	I
G	Draw up rota for checking and cleaning procedures	I
H	Establish procedures for maintenance of gym equipment	I
I	Draw up rota for checking equipment	I
J	Draw up new list of classes	I
L	Recruit teachers for classes	8
M, O	Organize client care session	I
N	Set up appointments system for gym during peak periods	I
P	Run client care session	Half-day
Q	Establish system for client care in gym	2
R	Organize and produce publicity brochure	6
S	Distribute brochure	2

If you now add times to the various activities in the logic diagram, you will see which route from Start to Finish will take the **longest** time. This route is the critical path – the **minimum** amount of time it will take to complete the project.

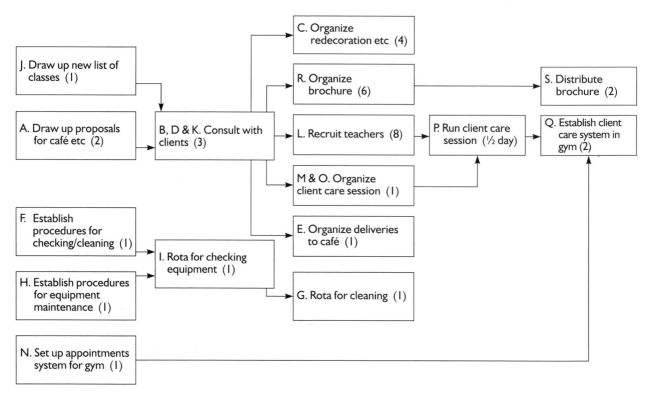

Critical path diagram for health club change project

In Stella's diagram, the critical path is A (2 weeks), B, D & K (three weeks), L (eight weeks), P (half a day) and Q (two weeks) – a total of 15 weeks. So if everything goes according to plan, the whole project should take less than four months. In reality, there could be some slippage. It may, for example, take more than eight weeks to recruit all the teachers. However, the diagram does establish the basis for week-by-week planning and monitoring.

Activity 28

8 mins

You can practise producing your own logic and critical path diagrams by starting with something simple, such as preparing a meal. Imagine you are asked to prepare the following menu:

- scrubbed and boiled new potatoes;
- cheese omelette;
- salad with dressing;
- strawberries and cream.

Draw a logic diagram and then a critical path diagram with the time for each task in minutes.

The task that is going to take the longest time in this menu is scrubbing and boiling the new potatoes. In fact, it is probable that this task alone will constitute your critical path. Parallel to it will be all the other tasks. All you need to do is work out how long each one is going to take and the best order in which to do them, ending with cooking the omelette.

5.3 Gantt charts

A Gantt chart, which is often in the form of a bar chart, shows all the key activities and when they should begin or end. (The activities are listed down the left-hand side and the timescale appears across the top.) The chart doesn't, however, show the relationship between different activities as clearly as a critical path diagram.

A Gantt chart for Stella's project would look like the one on page 58.

In this chart, a number of activities are all shown starting in the first week. But in fact, if the main priority is to get all elements of the project completed by the time the publicity brochure is distributed, rather than making lots of small improvements over a period of time, there are a number of activities that could be completed as late as week 13 (Activities F, G, H, I and N). These activities have what is referred to as 'float'. This is shown on the chart by the addition of a line. It's also apparent that organizing the client care session for staff (Activity M) could begin earlier. This activity is therefore said to have 'slack'. It's always useful to have some activities with float or slack as they will give you some flexibility in the schedule, which will probably be much-needed.

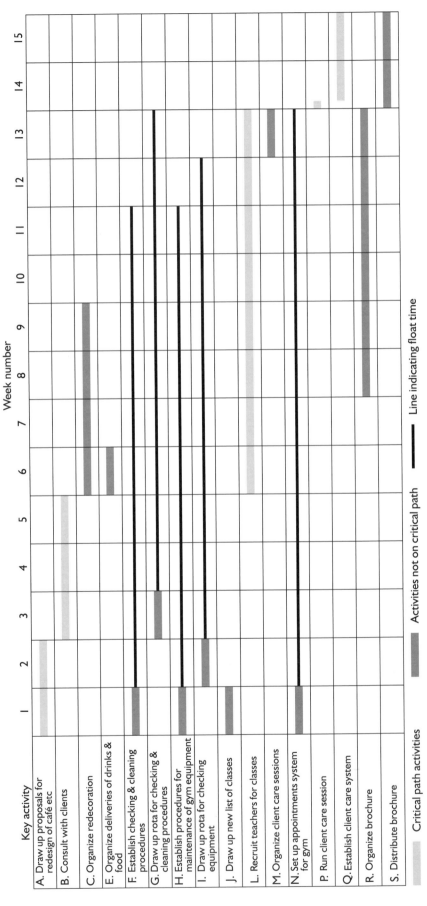

Gantt chart for health club change project

Key activity															
Week number	1	2	3	4	5	6	7	8	9	10	11	12	13	14	15

A. Draw up proposals for redesign of café etc

B. Consult with clients

C. Organize redecoration

E. Organize deliveries of drinks & food

F. Establish checking & cleaning procedures

G. Draw up rota for checking & cleaning procedures

H. Establish procedures for maintenance of gym equipment

I. Draw up rota for checking equipment

J. Draw up new list of classes

L. Recruit teachers for classes

M. Organize client care sessions

N. Set up appointments system for gym

P. Run client care session

Q. Establish client care system

R. Organize brochure

S. Distribute brochure

Critical path activities   Activities not on critical path   Line indicating float time

Activity 29

The health club project has several sub-projects, one of which is to produce and distribute a publicity brochure. The critical path analysis for this sub-project looks like this:

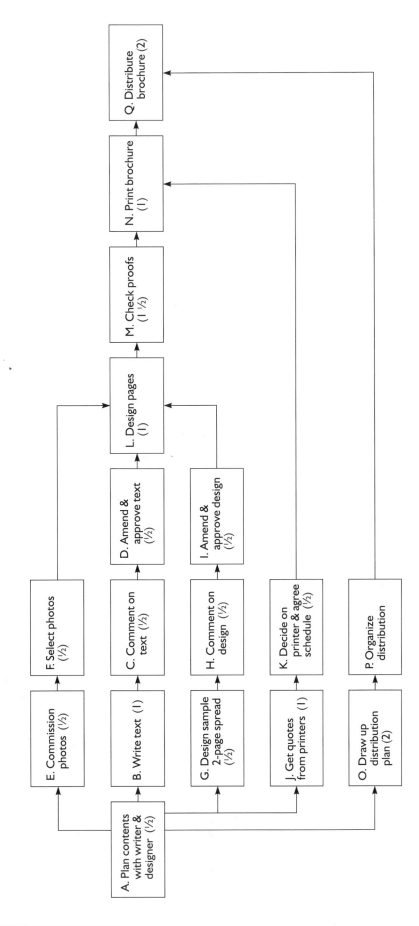

Try producing a Gantt chart for this sub-project using the outline overleaf. (Bear in mind that the printers may need to be informed at least a week before printing that they have been chosen to do the job.)

Week number

Activity	1	2	3	4	5	6	7	8
A								
B								
C								
D								
E								
F								
G								
H								
I								
J								
K								
L								
M								
N								
O								
P								
Q								

You can see a completed Gantt Chart on page 96.

Other information that can be added to a Gantt chart includes:

■ milestones (that is, special points where you think it's important to check on progress so far), perhaps represented by a diamond or triangle
■ project meetings, perhaps represented by a circle.

As you can see, it is a fairly easy task to draw a Gantt chart. However, computer software is available that will enable you to try out a number of different scenarios very quickly, showing what will happen if an activity takes a longer or shorter period of time than you originally forecast. Using the software will also make life much easier when it comes to monitoring the project's progress and making any necessary adjustments from week to week.

When drawing up a project plan, you need to bear in mind that plans have a tendency to go astray. So always aim to build some **contingency time** into your plan – and possibly some **contingency resources** – to help you cope with the unexpected. There are all sorts of ways in which things could go wrong for Stella: a vital staff member could fall ill; there may be a delay in the delivery of the furniture; there may be a problem with getting a piece of equipment fixed, and so on. Rather than telling the club owner that the project will be completed in under four months, she should make it clear that this is the **minimum** amount of time it will take.

6 Establishing responsibilities and methods of communication

As well as sorting out the key project activities and overall schedule, you need to establish exactly who is responsible for what. Whether you do this during the stage of planning the activities, or afterwards, will depend on the particular situation. However, whenever you do it, remember that if your team is to feel empowered, every member must have an established responsibility within the project.

Going back to Stella and the health club, for example, she would be making a big mistake if she thought she could manage all the key activities herself. In one of the initial team meetings it needs to be agreed exactly who will take responsibility for organizing the customer survey, who will take responsibility for sorting out the refurbishment of the café and reception area, and so on. In this particular example, the ideal time to do this may have been after the team had drawn up the logic diagram but before they started on the critical path diagram. However, this may not always be the case.

6.1 Identifying possible effects

Giving people new responsibilities not only means empowering them; it also means identifying what new skills they need to acquire. If they require further training, this may have the knock-on effect of an additional cost.

You will also need to consider the effects of the change not only on each member of your team, but also on the people outside your team – that is, the 'ripple' effects. It's essential that you discuss your plans for change with these people and together make an assessment of how they will be affected. You may need to consider ways of amending your plan to accommodate the requirements of people outside your team. Going through this process will have the added benefit of helping to break down any existing barriers between departments.

One major question to consider is: who is likely to resist the change, and how will you deal with this resistance? Never ignore signs of resistance or try to overcome it just by repeating arguments in support of change. Instead, attempt to understand the reasons for the resistance and be prepared to discuss these while pointing to the possible benefits of change for the individuals concerned. (You will find more on resistance to change, and how to respond to it, in another workbook in the series entitled *Understanding Change*.)

Activity 30

S/NVQ12.1

This Activity may provide the basis of appropriate evidence for your S/NVQ portfolio. If you are intending to take this course of action, write your answers on separate sheets of paper.

Look back at your notes in Activity 18b on a change project and consider the following questions:

a   How will each individual in your team be affected by the change?

_____

_____

b   What further training or development activities, if any, do they need to take part in?

_____

_____

c   Which other groups (if any) will be affected? How will they be affected?

_____

_____

d   What role should you play in dealing with these effects?

_____

_____

e   What are the likely effects (if any) on costs of all of the above?

_____

_____

6.2 Identifying lines and methods of communication

If the project is to run smoothly, you also need to ensure that there is good communication throughout. This means not only two-way communication between you and your team, but also keeping people outside the project informed about progress.

Activity 31 · 8 mins

S/NVQA1.3

This Activity may provide the basis of appropriate evidence for your S/NVQ portfolio. If you are intending to take this course of action, write your answers on separate sheets of paper.

Look back at your notes in Activity 18b on a change project and consider the following questions:

a Who are the people who need to be kept informed?

_____

_____

_____

b At what stages in the project should they be informed?

_____

_____

_____

c What are the best ways of informing them?

_____

_____

_____

64

The people who need to be kept informed will certainly include your manager. They may also include people in other departments or teams in your organization as well as all the members of your own team. The methods you use may include:

- memos and/or emails;
- regular written reports on progress, with reference to milestones;
- informal one-to-one conversations with your manager and team members;
- regular progress meetings with the whole team;
- ad hoc meetings with the team to sort out major problems as they arise.

It's a good idea to include team progress meetings in your schedule. However, never regard these as a substitute for other forms of communication. Rather, always be ready to listen and respond appropriately to the concerns voiced by members of your team and so keep up the team's morale.

We will return to the subject of communication in the next session.

Self-assessment 2

20 mins

For each of the statements 1 to 4, state whether it is TRUE or FALSE, and write a brief sentence explaining why.

1 Change that crosses departmental boundaries is always instigated by senior management. TRUE/FALSE

_____

_____

2 It is not enough to just 'sell' an idea for change to your staff. You must also empower them to control the necessary activities themselves. TRUE/FALSE

_____

_____

3 It isn't change that creates anxiety in staff so much as uncertainty about change. TRUE/FALSE

_____

_____

4 During a change project it is essential not to distract staff
from the job in hand by constantly providing them with
information.   TRUE/FALSE

T _____

_____

For questions 5 to 7, complete the sentences with a suitable word or words
from the following list:

SCOPE   ACTIVITIES   COMMUNICATION
TIMESCALE   RESOURCES   OBJECTIVES

5 The first step in planning a change project is to define the _____

of the project.

6 It's very important to establish the _____ of a project as early as

possible so that you know what you are setting out to achieve.

7 Once you have a rough idea of the project's _____ and the available

_____, you can begin to plan the _____.

8 Good _____ always helps a project to run smoothly.

For questions 9 to 11, circle the type of diagram that is being described.

9 This is in the form of a bar chart which shows all the key activities and when
they should begin or end.

LOGIC DIAGRAM/CRITICAL PATH DIAGRAM/GANTT CHART

10 This helps you to identify the key stages in a project and the order in which
they should occur.

LOGIC DIAGRAM/CRITICAL PATH DIAGRAM/GANTT CHART

11 This shows the relationship between different activities, identifying which
activities may run in parallel to each other and which must follow on
consecutively from each other.

LOGIC DIAGRAM/CRITICAL PATH DIAGRAM/GANTT CHART

12 In a Gantt chart some activities have 'slack', while others have 'float'. Which of the following statements about these terms are correct?

a   An activity is said to have 'float' if its completion date could be earlier than that shown in the chart. CORRECT/NOT CORRECT

b   Float is shown on the chart by the addition of a line. CORRECT/NOT CORRECT

c   An activity is said to have 'slack' if its completion date could be later than that shown in the chart. CORRECT/NOT CORRECT

d   Slack is shown on the chart by the addition of a line. CORRECT/NOT CORRECT

7 Summary

- There are many aspects to the role of a first line manager in change. They include:

  - instigating change;
  - calculating costs;
  - determining feasibility;
  - feeding back information to management;
  - keeping the team informed;
  - working out a strategy for deployment of staff;
  - coping with keeping things running during the change.

- It's important for a first line manager to win the support of their team for a proposed change. This means:

  - 'selling' the idea of change to the team;
  - empowering the team to cope with the change;
  - providing the team with the feeling of ownership of the change.

- A major change can be treated as a project or number of projects.

- The first steps in planning a change project are to establish the scope of the change and its aims and objectives.

- The next steps in project planning are to:

  - establish the approximate timescale and financial constraints within which you are working:
  - establish what staff and other resources you will need or are available to you;
  - identify the main project activities.

- Tools to help you in planning how you are going to achieve a project's aims and objectives are:

  - logic diagrams;
  - critical path diagrams;
  - Gantt charts.

- Constructing a logic diagram will help you to identify the key stages in a project and the order in which they should occur.

- A critical path diagram shows the relationship between different activities, identifying which activities may run in parallel to each other and which must follow on consecutively from each other.

- A Gantt chart is a bar chart that shows all the key activities in a project and when they should begin and end. Computer software is available that will not only help you to draw Gantt charts but also try out different scenarios very quickly.

- Once the project activities have been planned, you need to establish responsibilities. You also need to ensure that there will be effective communication both within your team and with people outside it.

Session C
Implementing change and managing its consequences

1 Introduction

We all know that in real life not everything goes according to plan. This means that when you implement a change project plan, you must be ready to:

- undertake thorough monitoring throughout the project;
- make adjustments to plans.

The good news is that if you have been thorough in your initial planning, this dual task of monitoring and making adjustments will be a lot easier.

However, no amount of planning can make dealing with the mixed emotions that change can arouse in people any easier. There may well be times when you will need all your interpersonal skills to cope with signs of stress among your staff. And you will certainly need not only to maintain your own enthusiasm for change wherever possible, but also to communicate this enthusiasm to others.

Even when a change project comes to an end, your role in managing change is not over. Remember, it's always important to acknowledge what has been achieved and celebrate this with staff – even if it's clear that you will soon be embarking on further change.

2 Monitoring the project plan

The first thing to note about monitoring is that it is impossible to carry it out unless you have good communication. It is only through communication that you will learn how the project is progressing and whether adjustments have to be made to the plan to deal with any deviations.

The monitoring process generally consists of the following stages:

- collect information, mainly from team members;
- check progress against plan and identify any deviations;
- identify the cause of any deviations and find solutions;
- when necessary, gain approval for changes in plan;
- implement solutions to bring the project back on track.

2.1 Types of deviation from the plan

One of the most common types of deviation you can expect to find is the amount of time spent on an activity. At the beginning of a project it's very easy to be over-optimistic about how much can be achieved in a particular amount of time. Of course, sometimes you are set an ultimate deadline and have no choice but to try and achieve it – even when you know it's going to be very difficult to do so. On the other hand, the amount of time allotted to activities in the planning of a project may not be unduly optimistic, and the only reason that an activity is not completed when it's supposed to be is poor time management.

One way of dealing with slippages in the schedule can be to employ more resources, whether they be in the form of people, equipment or materials. However, a lack of resources may in itself be a cause of deviation. Suddenly finding yourself without vital staff for whatever reason can throw the best-laid plan into confusion, and some people with particular skills are very difficult to replace at short notice.

Imagine, for example, a pub that is relying on an excellent, recently employed, chef to help restore the reputation of its restaurant and so build up its customer base. The owner has initiated a small change project with the aim of reaching a certain weekly profit. If the chef suddenly has to take time off work, what can the pub owner do when the agency chef sent to replace him turns out to be bad at his job? He may decide that it's actually better to close the restaurant for a few days, and delay achieving his goal, rather than jeopardize the whole project by serving customers with low-quality meals.

This brings us to something else that can go wrong with projects: the quality of the outcomes at certain stages. It may sometimes be necessary, as a last resort, to accept a reduction in the quality of an activity's outcome if this is the only way to get the project back on track. Suppose, for example, that part of the pub owner's change project is to improve the garden. He may have imagined a wonderful display of flowers and then found that certain plants fail to flourish because of the poor soil. In such a situation the best strategy is to revise his plans for the garden!

In short, you'll find that deviation from a project plan occurs most often in:

■ the time spent on activities;
■ the resources used;
■ the quality of activity outcomes.

Activity 32

S/NVQ C12.1

This Activity may provide the basis of appropriate evidence for your S/NVQ portfolio. If you are intending to take this course of action, it might be better to write your answers on separate sheets of paper.

Look back at the notes you wrote in Activity 18a regarding a change project in which you and your team have been involved.

■ What deviations from the plan occurred?

_____

_____

■ What measures did you or anybody else take to put the plan back on track?

_____

_____

2.2 Tracking progress

Keeping track of where you are in your plan is a lot easier if you have produced a critical path diagram and Gantt chart. This is particularly so if you have used computer software to produce your Gantt chart. You can then make any necessary adjustments to your chart as you go along and leave the software to reveal what the possible knock-on effects might be. To see how helpful a Gantt chart can be, let's return to the publicity brochure for the health club.

> At the beginning of week 5 of the project, Stella begins to organize the new publicity brochure. She has already warned the copy-writer and designer who normally work on the club's promotional literature that a new brochure is required, so she doesn't expect any problems in the early stages. However, when she rings up the copy-writer to ask him to come in for a meeting she discovers that he is in the middle of desperately trying to meet a deadline for another project and would like to delay their meeting for a week. Stella feels she has no alternative but to agree.
>
> Stella next rings the designer to arrange for her to come to the same meeting as the copy-writer. This is no problem. However, when the meeting takes place, Stella discovers that the designer is due to go on holiday for a week in three weeks' time. Will this mean that the brochure will end up delaying the 'Finish' date of the whole project? Looking at the Gantt chart and making a couple of adjustments will give her the answer.

Activity 33

Have a look at the Gantt chart you produced for Activity 29. If you make the adjustments that allow for the delayed meeting with the copy-writer and for the designer's holiday, what will the knock-on effects be?

■ When will the brochure be ready to go to the printer?

_____

■ Will the brochure be distributed before the agreed project 'Finish' date? If not, how late will it be?

_____

Delaying the initial meeting with the copy-writer by one week – so that it takes place in week 7 rather than week 6 – adds a week to the schedule. The designer's holiday in week 10 adds another week. This means the brochure will go to the printer in week 12 rather than week 10. This is fine, as the brochure is not due to be distributed until week 14. However, if there is any further slippage, the project will not be completed on time. It will become necessary for Stella to make some additional plans, such as getting either the copy-writer or designer to work late in the evening or at the weekend.

2.3 Identifying problems

In monitoring a project it's always helpful to have some idea about the types of problem that might arise. They could be to do with:

- staff – key people not being there when needed because of, for example, illness;
- physical resources – buildings, equipment or materials being defective in some way;
- technology – systems not working as they are supposed to;
- finance – promised money not being available after all, or various activities within the project going over budget;
- procedures – a process not going as expected.

Whatever the nature of the problem, you may have to undertake some serious problem solving with your team. This could entail:

- collecting whatever information is necessary to define the problem correctly;
- identifying possible causes;
- identifying possible solutions;
- choosing the best solution;
- implementing and evaluating the solution.

Another workbook in this series, *Solving Problems*, gives far more detail than we've got space for here. Suffice it to say here that among the tools you can use to help analyse the causes of problems is the **fishbone** or **cause and effect diagram** that we looked at in Session A.

If you look at a critical path diagram for a project, you may well be able to identify various points at which problems are particularly likely to arise.

Activity 34 · 3 mins

Take another look at the critical path diagram for the health club project on page 56. If you were Stella, what are the points at which you would want to keep a particularly close watch for problems?

There are a number of possible answers to this question. However, it's fair to say that one obvious point at which there could be problems is after the consultation with clients. As a general rule, activities that follow a merge need to be watched closely, as do activities that:

- are expected to take a long time to complete (such as the recruitment of teachers for the health club);
- have little or no float or slack (such as the drawing up of proposals for the café and reception area);
- involve a lot of people (such as establishing a client care system in the gym);
- involve new technology (as the appointments and client care systems might do if it was decided to computerize them);
- require people to do something they haven't done before (again, as in establishing a client care system in the gym).

2.4 Evaluating the project

Going hand in hand with the monitoring of a project is evaluation. While monitoring is about comparing what actually happened with what was planned, evaluation goes one step further and involves drawing conclusions about:

- what has been achieved;
- what has gone well or badly;
- why things have gone the way they have;
- what can be done better next time.

Evaluation does not all have to be done at the end of a project. In fact, it is best done at pre-defined points in a project's life. Lessons can then be learned and acted upon as the project progresses.

Activity 35 · 5 mins

Imagine you are in Stella's position at the health club. You decide that a good point at which to evaluate what has happened so far is after two subgroups of three people have drawn up the proposals for the café and reception area, and produced a list of classes. What could you hope to learn from the evaluation that you might feed back into the subsequent stages of the project?

_____

_____

_____

One of the basic things you might hope to learn is how efficient each of the subgroups is in meeting a deadline for completing a task such as drawing up proposals. After talking to members of the two groups, you might also discover who is more likely to act as a leader, who has good organizing talents, who is particularly committed to establishing a broad range of classes, and so on. This information can then be used to ensure that the most suitable people take on basic organizational tasks, such as setting up rotas, while the person particularly committed to expanding the classes becomes the one responsible for recruiting teachers.

3 Completing a change project

How do you know when a change project is completed? One obvious answer might be: 'When the final activity in the project plan has been completed' Another might be: 'When all the objectives have been met'. However, in reality, the original objectives and planned activities may have to be amended as the project evolves and as factors arise that are outside the control of you and your team – such as developments in the external environment. Furthermore, even the achievement of SMART objectives is not always possible to assess straight away. Suppose, for example, that one of the objectives of the health club project is that 'All clients in the gym should have their exercise needs assessed on a weekly basis'. It will take a few weeks for this to be put into practice and for data to be collected on whether, in fact, clients' needs are being properly assessed. And then various steps might have to be taken to improve the assessment of needs.

In fact, in the majority of change projects it's best never to think of them as ever totally completed. (There are notable exceptions to this rule – as when the change is a change of premises.) Generally speaking, there is always room for improvement, as was emphasized in Session A. Once the final activity in a project plan has been carried out, the best course is to keep on monitoring the outcomes and collect feedback that can be used as the basis for a programme of continual improvement.

At the same time you need to find a way of acknowledging your team's achievements in a change project and joining your team in some form of celebration. Different teams celebrate in different ways. Some take a night out together; others are happy to be allowed time for 'pet' projects. You could send a letter of thanks, addressed either to the team as a whole, or to each person individually. It is very important to show appreciation for an endeavour above and beyond the call of normal duty.

Activity 36 · 5 mins

S/NVQ A1.1

This Activity may provide the basis of appropriate evidence for your S/NVQ portfolio. If you are intending to take this course of action, it might be better to write your answers on separate sheets of paper.

Look back at the notes you wrote in Activity 18a regarding a change project in which you and your team have been involved.

■ At what point, if any, did you or your manager acknowledge that the project's main aims had been achieved?

_____

■ Having made this acknowledgment, were there any follow-on activities aimed at achieving further improvement? If so, what were they? If not, are there any follow-on activities that you think should have taken place?

_____

_____

3.1 Change fatigue

As well as acknowledging people's achievements, you also need to recognize that after a period of sustained effort, people often feel flat and tired. The completion of the final activity in the project plan may come as something of an anticlimax. Time is needed to recover: nobody can work at an intense level for long without a period of recuperation.

Unfortunately, this is not always recognized, with the result that in some workplaces people suffer from what is known as 'change fatigue'. They begin to feel that change is being instigated for its own sake, and without any apparent overall plan. As change after change takes place, they naturally become reluctant to co-operate, wondering when the latest project will be supplanted by another one.

Activity 37 ·

Have you ever suffered from change fatigue? Apart from stopping the programme of change, was there any particular action by management that may have helped to alleviate it?

_____

_____

_____

Your answer to the question in Activity 37 will depend on your particular circumstances. However, there is one general rule that all managers at all levels can follow where there is a danger of change fatigue: keep staff informed about why change is necessary from the earliest possible date.

3.2 Life after redundancies

A theme throughout this workbook has been that change is necessary and has many benefits for both organizations and individual staff alike. However, there are some types of change in organizations that can have adverse effects on people, the most obvious of which is redundancy.

We hear a lot about the trauma suffered by people who have been made redundant. This is understandable. Security of employment hardly exists any more, and we are naturally sympathetic when someone suddenly finds himself or herself without a job. To go through a career without having been made redundant seems to be an exceptional feat these days.

Another problem that is very real, but which is given far less publicity, is that of the employees left behind after a 'pruning down' of staff numbers. The survivors of redundancy often feel threatened, guilty and overworked, and they need special handling.

If you have ever found yourself in the position of managing a team following a spate of redundancies, you will know the importance of:

- building team cohesion and morale back up;
- returning work routines to normal as soon as possible;
- watching out for signs of stress;
- pacing the workload, so that the new team can quickly recover their sense of pride and achievement, and not become overwhelmed by the backlog piling up.

In the period immediately following the redundancies, it may be good policy to step up the rate of work, to get over the 'change crisis'. You may find that the team members feel they need to do more to help them get over their sense of guilt. However, it is usually a mistake to make that the norm.

Redundancies are often caused by restructuring programmes. Such programmes can give new responsibilities to the remaining staff – responsibilities that they do not always feel equipped to handle. One response to this situation can be to feel inadequate and stressed; another can be to see it as a welcome opportunity to develop new skills. This can apply as much to first line managers as it does to team members.

Activity 38 · 5 mins

Have you ever been in a situation where a change programme required you to develop new skills? If you haven't, try to think of someone you know who has. What was your/their response?

_____

_____

_____

_____

What help were you given in developing these skills?

_____

_____

_____

_____

What did you/they learn from this experience about how to regard change in the future?

_____

_____

_____

_____

EXTENSIONS 2 and 3
An overview of what's involved in managing change is supplied by Extension 2, _Managing Change_ by Robert Heller. You will find more detailed accounts in Extension 3, _Harvard Business Review on Change_.

You may have had a negative experience, but hopefully you have learned that change is not something to avoid whenever possible. Rather, it has the potential to provide exciting new opportunities to develop the skills of both you and your staff and help your organization to prosper in a constantly changing environment.

Self-assessment 3

10 mins

1 Complete the following steps in the monitoring process with a suitable word chosen from the following list.

PLAN   INFORMATION   SOLUTIONS
DEVIATIONS   CHANGES   CAUSE

- Collect _____, mainly from team members

- Check progress against _____ and identify any _____

- Identify the _____ of any deviations and find solutions

- When necessary, gain approval for _____ in plan

- Implement _____ to bring the project back on track

2 The main types of problems that can arise during the implementation of projects are to do with staff, physical resources, technology, finance and procedures. Can you say a bit more about what these problems are likely to be?

- Staff

_____

_____

- Physical resources

_____

_____

- Technology

_____

_____

- Finance

_____

_____

■ Procedures

_____

_____

3   What process is described by each of the following?

a   It consists of drawing conclusions about what has been achieved, why things have gone the way they have, and what can be done better next time.

_____

b   It consists of identifying the reasons why something has gone wrong, and identifying and implementing a solution.

_____

c   It consists of comparing what has actually happened with what was planned and responding accordingly.

_____

4   Which of the following statements are good advice to the leader of a team that has just participated in a major change? What is wrong with the statements that you think are not good advice?

a   Always make a point of acknowledging what has been achieved.
b   Avoid celebrating the end of a change project when another change project is imminent.
c   Recognize that people may feel flat and tired after a project and give them time to recuperate.
d   If staff are suffering from change fatigue, cut down on the amount of information you give them about the next change project.
e   If the change has involved redundancies, bear in mind that the survivors may feel threatened and guilty.
f   Immediately after redundancies have been made, never increase the workload of the survivors.

_____

_____

_____

_____

_____

4 Summary

- Good communication is the key to monitoring change successfully.

- The most common forms of deviation from a plan for change are in:
  - the time spent on individual activities;
  - the resources used;
  - the quality of activity outcomes.

- Keeping track of progress is made a lot easier by the use of a critical path diagram and Gantt chart.

- Problems that arise during a change project may be to do with:
  - staff;
  - physical resources;
  - technology;
  - finance;
  - procedures.

- Going hand in hand with monitoring is evaluation, which involves drawing conclusions about:
  - what has been achieved;
  - what has gone well or badly;
  - why things have gone the way they have;
  - what can be done better next time.

- It's always important to mark the end of a change project in some way and, whenever possible, celebrate what has been achieved.

- Too much change can result in 'change fatigue'. People need time to recover after a major change project.

- Change involving redundancies can have an adverse effect on the survivors as well as on those made redundant. In such situations you will need to pay close attention to building up morale and pacing the workload.

- Change has the potential to provide exciting new opportunities for both you and your staff to develop new skills.

Performance checks

1 Quick quiz

Jot down the answers to the following questions on *Managing Change*.

Question 1 What is the Japanese name for continuous improvement?

_____

Question 2 Most small improvements in the workplace can be placed in one of four categories. Two of these are: the physical conditions in which you work, and resources. What are the other two categories?

_____

Question 3 What does the Five Whys technique consist of?

_____

_____

_____

Question 4 Why is flowcharting a helpful tool in identifying areas for improvement in a process?

_____

_____

_____

Question 5 In a cause and effect, or fishbone, diagram, what does the main horizontal arrow usually represent?

_____

Question 6   In a cause and effect, or fishbone, diagram, the small arrows represent inputs. Categories of inputs vary, but often include method (procedures) and environment (physical conditions). Can you name two others?

_____

Question 7   If three of the 5 Ss are Sort, Set in order and Shine, what are the other two?

_____

Question 8   Red tagging is a form of visual management. What does it consist of?

_____

_____

_____

Question 9   How does the setting of standards play a vital part in any programme of continuous improvement?

_____

_____

_____

Question 10   In managing change, what must the team leader do to ensure the full participation of the team in the change process.

_____

_____

_____

Question 11   In planning a change project you begin by defining the project's scope, aims and objectives. Is there anything else you need to establish before doing any detailed planning of the project activities?

_____

_____

Question 12   What does a critical path diagram show about the key activities in a project? What does a Gantt chart show?

_____

_____

_____

Question 13   What is the one thing that is essential to the successful monitoring of a plan?

_____

Question 14   Name one of the most common forms of deviation from a project plan.

Question 15   What is the main difference between monitoring and evaluation?

Answers to these questions can be found on pages 99–100.

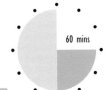

60 mins

2 Workbook assessment

Read the following example about someone identifying a possible improvement in a process which will affect other parts of the organization. Answer the questions below, writing your answers on a separate sheet of paper.

Ben works as the manager of the unit assembly team in a factory producing electrical heaters. When a 5S programme is introduced, it quickly became apparent that the difficulties Ben's team face amount to rather more than old and grubby benches. The various parts that are to be assembled arrive from different parts of the factory in boxes that take up a lot of space and are often difficult to unpack. Furthermore, there is sometimes a shortage of one or more parts.

When Ben starts to look into all this he realizes that a basic cause of the problem is that the various assembly activities are scattered around the factory. As far as he can see, it makes much more sense for plastic casing assembly, switch assembly, motor and fan assembly, and heater coil assembly to be brought together in one place with unit assembly. He decides to arrange a meeting with his manager to discuss his idea for improvement and what he should do about it.

Imagine you are Ben's manager. What advice will you give him in this and subsequent meetings about:

■ what he should do before he even begins to consider drawing up a proposal for change;
■ what tasks he should undertake in drawing up a proposal for change;
■ whom he should discuss his ideas with and how he should go about winning their support for change.

Your complete answer to this assessment need not be longer than a single page.

3 Work-based assignment

S/NVQ C12.1

The time guide for this assignment gives you an approximate idea of how long it is likely to take you to write up your findings. You will find you need to spend some additional time gathering information, talking to colleagues and thinking about the assignment. The results of your efforts should be presented on separate sheets of paper.

The assignment may provide the basis of appropriate evidence for your S/NVQ portfolio. The assignment is designed to help you demonstrate:

■ your teambuilding skills;
■ your ability to focus on results;
■ your ability to take decisions;
■ your ability to influence others.

What you have to do

For this assignment, identify a fairly major change that you expect to happen in the near future. If you wish, return to the change that you first identified in Activity 18b (and subsequently considered in Activities 23, 25, 26, 30 and 31).

Write a few sentences defining the scope of the project (and the date by which it is to be completed if this is known). Then, consulting with members of your team wherever possible, carry out the following:

■ Draw up a list of aims and objectives for your team in implementing the change. Wherever possible, make the objectives:

  – specific;
  – measurable;
  – achievable;
  – relevant;
  – timebound.

  (Bear in mind that it may not always be possible to produce SMART objectives until you have done more detailed planning. However, you should be able to identify the main aims of the project.)

■ Draw up a list of the main activities that your team must undertake in order to achieve the objectives. (Aim to keep this list as short as possible – a maximum of 12 activities would be ideal for this assignment.)

■ Establish what resources you need to complete these activities in terms of:

  – staff (including hours, abilities and skills);
  – other resources (such as equipment);
  – approximate budget.

■ Establish whether any of your team members will require additional training or development to acquire the necessary skills.

What you should write

■ Write a concise project outline that contains the following information:

  – the project's scope;
  – aims and objectives;
  – timescale (which may only be approximate at this initial stage);
  – necessary resources, including staff time, abilities and skills;
  – any necessary additional training or development for staff;
  – budget (which again may only be approximate at this initial stage).

■ Draw the following diagrams to help you plan the project:

  – a logic diagram (which begins with 'Start' and ends with 'Finish' but has no timescale and focuses on showing which activities are dependent on other activities);
  – a critical path diagram (which shows how long individual activities will take and the chain of activities that will take the longest time between 'Start' and 'Finish');
  – a Gantt chart (showing the activities and timescale, plus possible milestones where you think it will be important to check on progress to date).

■ Once you have completed your diagrams, write a concise paragraph explaining how you might use them in implementing and monitoring the change project.

■ Finally, write a brief paragraph on communication throughout the project, stating whom you will need to keep informed on progress and problems, and the methods you will use for doing this.

The written part of this document does not have to be more than two or three pages long. You will probably need a separate sheet of paper for each diagram.

Reflect and review

1 Reflect and review

Now that you have completed your work on *Managing Change*, let's review our workbook objectives. First:

■ You will be better able to initiate improvements in workplace activities.

There is always scope for improvement in any of the following:

- the physical conditions in which you and your staff work;
- the resources you and your staff work with;
- the relationships you have with other people both within and outside the organization;
- the procedures you and your staff follow.

If you make a point of always being on the look-out for possible improvements in any of these areas, you will be contributing to a process of continuous improvement – something that more and more organizations are considering essential to their continuing success and prosperity.

Of course, there is more to initiating improvements than just identifying where they are needed. Before taking any action you may have to investigate the root cause of a problem, using such tools as flowcharts, cause and effect diagrams and the Five Whys.

You may want to ask yourself the following questions regarding these points:

■ How can I ensure that I identify areas for improvement on a continual basis and actually do something about them?

_____

_____

_____

■ Do I feel confident about using the tools described in this workbook for identifying the root causes of problems? If not, how might I go about building up this confidence, and perhaps even learning about other tools associated with continuous improvement?

_____

_____

_____

The second workbook objective was:

■ You will be better able to plan change projects.

A huge amount of work can go into planning major change. In fact, in some cases it's better to think of a major change as a number of projects rather than one. Whatever the size of the project, there are always certain processes that you will need to go through, such as:

■ collecting information;
■ establishing the aims and objectives;
■ establishing the timescale and necessary resources (including budget and staff);
■ assessing the feasibility of the project;
■ identifying the necessary activities and planning the order in which they are to be done, and by whom.

There are various tools you can use in planning projects, such as critical path diagrams and Gantt charts. For larger projects you will find them indispensable.

INSTITUTE OF LEADERSHIP & MANAGEMENT

SUPERSERIES

Managing Change

....

has satisfactorily completed this workbook

Name of signatory ....

Position ....

Signature ....

Date ....

Official stamp

Fourth Edition

INSTITUTE OF LEADERSHIP & MANAGEMENT
SUPERSERIES
FOURTH EDITION

Achieving Quality	0 7506 5874 6
Appraising Performance	0 7506 5838 X
Becoming More Effective	0 7506 5887 8
Budgeting for Better Performance	0 7506 5880 0
Caring for the Customer	0 7506 5840 1
Collecting Information	0 7506 5888 6
Commitment to Equality	0 7506 5893 2
Controlling Costs	0 7506 5842 8
Controlling Physical Resources	0 7506 5886 X
Delegating Effectively	0 7506 5816 9
Delivering Training	0 7506 5870 3
Effective Meetings at Work	0 7506 5882 7
Improving Efficiency	0 7506 5871 1
Information in Management	0 7506 5890 8
Leading Your Team	0 7506 5839 8
Making a Financial Case	0 7506 5892 4
Making Communication Work	0 7506 5875 4
Managing Change	0 7506 5879 7
Managing Lawfully – Health, Safety and Environment	0 7506 5841 X
Managing Lawfully – People and Employment	0 7506 5853 3
Managing Relationships at Work	0 7506 5891 6
Managing Time	0 7506 5877 0
Managing Tough Times	0 7506 5817 7
Marketing and Selling	0 7506 5837 1
Motivating People	0 7506 5836 3
Networking and Sharing Information	0 7506 5885 1
Organizational Culture and Context	0 7506 5884 3
Organizational Environment	0 7506 5889 4
Planning and Controlling Work	0 7506 5813 4
Planning Training and Development	0 7506 5860 6
Preventing Accidents	0 7506 5835 5
Project and Report Writing	0 7506 5876 2
Securing the Right People	0 7506 5822 3
Solving Problems	0 7506 5818 5
Storing and Retrieving Information	0 7506 5894 0
Understanding Change	0 7506 5878 9
Understanding Finance	0 7506 5815 0
Understanding Quality	0 7506 5881 9
Working In Teams	0 7506 5814 2
Writing Effectively	0 7506 5883 5

To order – phone us direct for prices and availability details
(please quote ISBNs when ordering) on 01865 888190